Competing in Cross-Country Skiing

B.H. Nilsson

A Drake Publication
STERLING PUBLISHING CO., INC. NEW YORK

Oak Tree Press Co., Ltd.
London & Sydney

Translated by Maxine Hobson

Revised Edition 1979

Two Park Avenue, New York, N.Y. 10016
Originally published under the title "Fondo—Sciare Come al Nord"

Manufactured in the United States of America

Library of Congress Catalog Card No.: 74-82340
Sterling/Drake ISBN 0-8069-8866-5
Sterling ISBN 0–8069-4076-X Trade
4077–8 Library
Oak Tree 7061–2655-6 Paper
2024-8 Trade

Contents

This photo, from 1945, shows Nils Karlsson of Sweden, known as the "king of cross-country" in his time, headed for victory in that year's 50-km. Swedish Championship race.

In Scandinavia, Skiing Means "Cross-Country"

To ski means to move across snow-covered ground with the aid of skis. It is a simple concept which, however, presents different aspects depending upon who is talking about it—people from the flatter north or from mountainous countries. The thoughts of the latter fly to steep slopes mantled in snow where it is possible to ski for miles and miles, descending over well-travelled trails, returning to the summit with little effort thanks to funiculars, chair lifts or ski tows.

Even in the north, certainly, in the Scandinavian countries, are mountains that are tall enough for downhill skiing, but the length and steepness of their descents are not comparable to those of the Alps or the Rocky Mountains. Even where this kind of skiing is possible, there is often a lack of access roads, much less means of ascent. Moreover, in Scandinavia, the snow covers not only the mountains but, for a good part of the winter, it falls abundantly on the vast plains and among the woods, covering the entire land right up to the edge of the sea. The large cities like Oslo, Stockholm and Helsinki are subject to heavy snows and, sometimes, if it is not cleared away quickly, you can see children on skis in the streets right in the middle of town.

For the Scandinavians, skis have always represented a practical means of getting themselves quickly from one place to another. Skis were, in fact, ideal for moving along the bad streets of an earlier time, much better than traversing them with a horse or a wagon. And thanks to the use of skis, it was and is possible to traverse terrain impassable by other

A typical cross-country touring party.

means during the cold season. The structure of the Swedish countryside is very different from more densely populated countries. Elsewhere we find streets, paths and houses at every step. In Sweden, on the other hand, great forests and thousands of lakes impede rapid movement from one point to the other. The houses of a community are sparse, spread over a large area and people are scarce. This is why the Nordic people think of skiing not only as a pleasant pastime but also as a means of communication. In contemporary sporting parlance, this method of skiing is called "cross-country" or "Nordic" to distinguish it from the other, that practiced in the Alps and elsewhere, with the name of "downhill."

Cross-country skiing as an established sport is relatively young. The first organized race was held at the end of the last century: it was only then that the daring and skill of skiers competing over fixed-distance, deliberately prepared courses came to be recognized. Even before that, stories were told of men who had carried off great feats on skis, but these were not competitions as we understand them. They were, rather, tales of legendary efforts of men on skis who had covered great distances in short time—greater than those set forth in the sports rules today, for example, the 50-kilometre (31-mile) race which is the longest cross-country race in men's Olympic competition. The other men's events are 15-km. (9.3-mi.) and 30-km. (18.6-mi.) races plus a 40-km. (24.8-mi.) relay. The women's cross-country events are 5-km. (3.1-mi.) and 10-km. (6.2-mi.) races plus a 15-km. (9.3-mi.) relay.

LEGENDARY SKIERS

In Scandinavia today, they still talk about old-time wolf hunts on skis that lasted many days and covered hundreds of miles. Grandparents tell their grandchildren a story about a violinist who lived 150 years ago in Lima, Sweden (the birthplace of Sixten Jernberg, two-time winner of the Olympic 50-kilometre race). This violinist was invited to play at a wedding, but he broke a violin string. He decided to go to Elverum, Norway, the closest city where he could find a new string and off he went on his skis. Returning the next day just in time to play for the wedding dance, he had had to ski 180 kilometres (108 miles)!

Another renowned skier was Gustav Eriksson Vasa (1496–1560) who became king of Sweden. In 1520, Sweden was ruled by a Danish king. Gustav, known for his great patriotism, was imprisoned in a castle in Denmark, but he managed to escape, and eventually reached Mora, in Sweden. Here, near his birthplace, he tried to persuade the people to rise up against the enemy. Disappointed at finding little enthusiasm for his ideas, Gustav continued his flight, going toward the Norwegian border,

Military drill on skis—a Scandinavian print from the 19th century.

pursued again by Danish soldiers. Meanwhile, after much discussion, the people of Mora convinced themselves of the necessity for revolting against the usurper and decided to send two messengers to bring the patriot back to give life and leadership to the revolution. Two of the best skiers in Mora set out and caught up with Gustav in Sälen, a town near the Norwegian border. Returning to Mora, the brave Swedish soldier gathered support and, in short order, succeeded in driving the Danes out of Sweden. In 1523, Gustav Eriksson Vasa was crowned king of Sweden and reigned as Gustav I.

Four hundred years later, in 1923, Swedish sportsmen, in memory of the deed of Gustav Eriksson and the two swift skiers from Mora, established the "Wasalopp," or Vasa Race, an 86-kilometre (53-mile) cross-country skiing contest from Sälen to Mora. It has become what is, perhaps, the most popular cross-country trial in the world, and was run in 1973 for the 50th time. In recent years, an incredible number of participants have taken part in this contest: more than 10,000 entrants, including many non-Swedes.

Unlike other cross-country races, the participants all start out at the same time in the Wasalopp: no other race in the world provides such a fantastic show.

Sweden's famous Wasalopp—a multicolored necklace glides silently through the marshes and woods of the Sälen-Mora course.

SKIS OF THE PAST

In re-examining the deeds which brought fame to the skiers of the past, it is interesting to consider also the equipment with which they prepared themselves to face their snowy challenges. The skis, poles, boots, wax—in short, the basic equipment—in general use in cross-country has undergone a great, continuing evolution from the beginning of competition at the end of the 19th century until today.

An ancient leather-covered hunting ski and a remnant of an ornately decorated ski from the 18th century.

The models in active use today, particularly those used in a 50-kilometre race, are not the same as the skis in fashion 20 to 50 years ago, much less those used 3,000 or 4,000 years ago. Those old-time skis were made not for competition but for travelling from one place to another, for hunting in the woods, or for the other demands of life at that time. The oldest skis known were much wider than today's skis, measuring between 15 and 25 centimetres (6 and 10 inches). One legend tells of a Viking who used his ski as a shield, it was so wide and thick. In more recent times, in contrast, skis were made very narrow and more than 3 metres (almost 10 feet) long. Today, cross-country skis are not more than 6 cm. ($2\frac{3}{8}$ in.) wide and vary in length from 2 metres 5 cm. to 2 metres 20 cm. (82 to 88 inches).

In those earlier times, ski poles as we know them didn't exist. Skiers used a hunting lance to give themselves a push and to maintain balance. This lance had a steel tip at one end while the other end was artistically carved wood or bone. The method of skiing with two poles probably started with the first cross-country race.

The first bindings were simply straps which bound the foot directly to the wood. Another early, practical type of binding was made of a hoop or ring fastened perpendicularly through the middle of the ski in such a way that the toe of the shoe could be put through it. The toes of shoes were curled up in those days which prevented the shoes from sliding out during movement, while still allowing the foot to lift up and come down in order to give motion to the ski.

Ski wax also originated long ago and was extremely important since people skied with only one pole. To overcome the problem of sliding backwards, early skiers resorted to the expedience of covering their skis with reindeer or elk hides, naturally giving up some speed. They got around this problem by constructing their two skis with different characteristics. One was long, of hard wood and very smooth and was used for gliding. The other was short and was all or partly covered with animal skin and was used for pushing. This ski was called "andur" which means "to go."

The invention had a disadvantage, however: the muscles in the part of the body involved with pushing, particularly those in the hip, developed more than those used only for gliding. The result was that the natural gait of the cross-country skier was ruined. In fact, when not on skis these skiers walked unevenly, compelled by habit. Nowadays we wouldn't think of calling anyone an athlete who has such an unbalanced way of walking that he seems deformed.

Woodcut print of an old Nordic skier with a short ski on one foot, a long one on the other. Note the strap bindings and the curved-point shoes.

Today every self-respecting skier has all the necessary equipment for training and for competition. With the great selection to choose from, each athlete has a particular preference for a particular brand that he insists on for the most important and difficult contests. Things were no different in the past, even when there was no talk about competition, championships or Olympic Games. Among the numerous early skis which have been preserved for us with extreme care are pairs that range from common, everyday types to more refined and decorated types that were used in grand celebrations. Some skis were made of special wood, very hard and smooth, the result of careful searching during the summer in the large forests of the region.

Skiing in Scandinavia is very important also from the standpoint of military defence. The Finnish divisions of ski troops aroused the admiration of the whole world when they were able to hold back the much larger number of Russian troops who invaded their land in the winter of 1939–40. This was possible because the detachments were made up of skiing soldiers, well trained, moving in ranks quickly and silently over

A collection of antique skis and boots. The upturned points of the boots were inserted into the bindings. Some of these skis were dug up in marshes and may be more than a thousand years old.

the otherwise impassable expanse of snow. This wasn't the Russians first encounter with ski troops in a war. At the beginning of the 17th century, the Swedes were obliged to fight them to defend their land.

FAMILY SPORT

After being for centuries a useful practice in everyday life in Scandinavia, skiing has now become a world-wide sport and pastime. Although downhill skiing is gaining popularity in Scandinavia, especially among the young, the phenomenon is hardly started. The Scandinavians are still for the most part passionate about cross-country and their techniques serve as a model for the rest of the world. This sport is not developed over long descents but rather over flat and sometimes ascending ground, and it obliges its followers to put forth all the strength and resistance of their bodies over mile after mile of uneven ground. One reason, of course, for the enthusiasm for Nordic skiing is the opportunity to do it. The terrain of many regions does not offer another alternative. On holidays entire families can go to nearby parks and woods for skiing recreation, for the pleasure of spending several hours in contact with nature. They don't use the heavy laminated skis required for downhill, and it isn't necessary to use safety bindings. The skis are very much lighter and the bindings serve only to attach the end of the shoe to the wood allowing the foot free movement as in ordinary walking. Elaborate apparel isn't necessary and doesn't follow the whims of the latest styles. It isn't necessary to go up to a high altitude to put on skis and much cross-country is done near sea level. Cross-country is even easier to do at

At this age, it is possible for everyone to compete.

Concentration before a race is intense, even when it is not an Olympic medal at stake.

low altitude than higher where there is less oxygen, the air is rarefied, and recreation becomes a great expenditure of energy. It is unusual to come across cross-country skiers in high mountains.

For Scandinavian children, skis are their most popular toy: snow is right on the doorstep of their homes and it can be said that the young Swedes, Finns and Norwegians take their first steps with skis on their feet. At 7 or 8 years old they start competing: the runs are very short, and they usually compete without the aid of poles. At this age they don't use regular training methods, but since the children have to ski to get to school, the preparation comes automatically. As the children get older they approach competition in the sport with a technique already acquired and a naturalness of movement important to methodical preparation. This explains a good share of the superiority Nordic cross-country skiers have shown in the past compared to those who tried to bring down their supremacy.

For people in countries with enough mountains to have developed a tradition of downhill skiing, it is, naturally, difficult to understand this love which the northern people have for the sport of cross-country. Cross-country, however, lets you enjoy nature, skiing in woods and valleys that are always different. Whoever does downhill always sees the same

Some day he may race for a medal, but for now, the joy of competition is enough.

trails and risks, moreover, breaking his neck if he isn't well trained. Cross-country can also be practiced by a skier who is not very skillful because the exercise can be limited in relation to the skier's own strength; legs not accustomed to stress risk less at cross-country than legs in the same condition on a downhill course. Cross-country skiing is hard, but you get satisfaction more nearly equal to the amount of energy you consume.

It isn't, in fact, necessary to ski 50 km. (30 mi.) to have fun; a much shorter distance will do. The skis run without exertion over the snow, your heart and lungs speeding up in their work in a healthy atmosphere. Your body, forced by daily living and by the needs which encompass it and an inactivity that isn't healthy, cannot do other than to respond positively.

Why Not Begin Training?

Of all the skiers who train, very few have the chance to participate in the Olympics or in other truly important competitions. Even so, many men and women, young and old, do cross-country without the ambition to win a gold medal. They do it for entertainment, for physical exercise, to enjoy nature, to take long tours in the mountains, to meet other

Long-distance races give amateurs a good opportunity to test their strength and stamina.

people, for the excitement of taking part in amateur competitions and there are many other reasons why they are inspired to train.

Competition for amateurs has had great success in the last years, especially long-distance competition in which professionals also participate. A typical example is the Wasalopp with its thousands of participants in recent years. In competitions like the Wasalopp, few of the participants enter with the idea of winning. For most, the great "victory" is reaching the finish line after 86 kilometres. It doesn't make any difference whether you place 5,335th or 5,336th, the important thing is having run the 86 km. (53 mi.) and surely each one who finishes the Wasalopp is satisfied with the result.

There is another reason why cross-country is so popular, and it is perhaps the most important. Today people want to keep in shape without being athletes. Most work in offices or have occupations that give them little

This is hardly the competition for first place, but even so, there is tension in the air. Each competitor is hoping that neither of his skis is broken.

physical exercise, so they practice a sport to stay agile and to keep them from getting fat. Cross-country is perfect in this sense: the equipment isn't expensive and you can train for it all year long. Not always on natural snow, perhaps, but according to modern experts it is essential for competitors to train year round and for amateurs, too, it is useful to do a little advance training in the seasons without snow. Naturally an amateur who has a job, a family and other personal obligations isn't able to train like a professional. To be an Olympic skier today means an obligation to put in long periods of training and to like the travelling that this career

Pre-season training for the winter races. These photos are of Sweden's Lidingöloppet, a 30-km. (18.6 mi.) race with thousands of participants of all ages.

entails. Training for an amateur is like that of the professional in every way except in the amount of time devoted. A professional must train 15–20 hours a week, while for the amateur 1–3 hours are enough. The amateur probably will not devote as many weeks to training as the professional. It is the concern of each to determine how many hours and how many weeks of the year to devote to his aims. Since the training of the amateur follows the same principles as that of the professional, the training rules that follow are valid for both.

Pay attention to the time devoted to training, to its intensity, and to the distance to be covered. If a champion begins by covering 10–15 km. (6–9 mi.) in pretraining, a beginner could start with 2–3 km. (about 1–2 mi.), perhaps even less. It is a matter of following a schedule that trains the body, especially the lungs and heart, for the attainment of a goal which could be as ambitious as participation in the Wasalopp or just the simple desire to stay in shape. An amateur should also equip himself like a professional. It isn't a question of possessing stylish clothes and skis, but of having the most suitable.

The first thing is appropriate clothing for pre-season training as well as for training on skis. Pay the most attention to the skis, the poles, and the wax. Then you need boots for pre-training and boots for skiing. The skis should be those made specifically for cross-country. Please don't try to go cross-country using downhill skis. You won't enjoy yourself, you'll spoil your feet and kill the desire to do cross-country. In case you are concerned about the cost of all this, be assured that the equipment is less costly than that for downhill skiing.

The Technique for Training on the First Snow

The courses for cross-country races have changed in recent years and techniques have changed a little as a result, for example, a greater use of ski poles. Also, double poling has come to be used more and competitors have to work actively for the entire duration of a race. A cross-country skier with little technique can win only if he is strong enough and if he has built up his heart and lungs. This doesn't mean that technique is not important for it is easy to find numerous athletes with the same strength of heart and lungs, but it is becoming ever more difficult to find them with good technical preparation. At one time, almost all champions started to ski at 3 or 4 years and from that age on, generally skied through the whole winter, and so attained a good technique with the passing of the years. By the age of 15, these youngsters had more than 10 years of practice and training and the technique was second nature for them. Today, however, few children have this chance. Every family has a car, there is too much traffic to allow skiing in the streets and, moreover, the cars spoil the snow. Children no longer go to school on skis because almost everywhere in the world, there are school buses or other transportation. As a result, would-be competitors are forced to work more on technique. During training a coach often meets athletes who are strong and well prepared but who will never become champions because of poor technique, or more precisely because their technique is not perfect. Training in technique is not a waste of time.

Inexpert skiers, as a rule, go to school not to learn cross-country skiing, but exercises for downhill. These exercises taken together, or each one alone, permit the student to perform downhill skiing of every type and difficulty.

The author, second from the left, with the medal-winning members of the Italian blue team who posed for the instructional photos in this section—Franco Nones, Giuseppe Steiner and Giulio de Florian.

Children almost always succeed in learning either downhill or cross-country without being taught by an instructor because of the facility they have for learning simple things by imitation. Almost all those who have become champion skiers acquired the basic elements of technique by themselves when they were little by watching people who could ski well. When children grow up, reaching or surpassing 15 or 16 years, the method of learning by watching others becomes more difficult. Not having a teacher or a trainer at hand means only losing precious time. This does not mean that a person cannot do the first steps alone, especially in cross-country.

Don't think, however, that you can do cross-country with downhill equipment. To accomplish long, pleasant excursions in the mountains or to ski over a marked cross-country course, you need to use lighter skis and bindings that don't block your heels so that your feet are free to move. This mobility is furthered by the shoes of light, soft leather made for cross-country, completely different from downhill boots. The boots presently used for cross-country competition are hardly sturdier than walking shoes.

Many people do find cross-country tiring and it can be really exhausting if you are not in good physical condition. But it is three times more tiring if you don't know the technique. When a skier doesn't know the proper method, he moves rigidly and with a great dispersion of strength.

Yes, people talk about good physical condition and athletic ability, and this is especially important for those who take part in competitive activities. Good preparation is the foundation for efficiency and it takes a considerable amount of time to acquire it.

For the ordinary devotees of cross-country, thorough training is helpful but it isn't indispensable as it is for the serious athlete. If you are not competing in a race, you are not obliged to go on for a long time at high speed, but can stop and rest whenever it is convenient. You can ski along slowly with pleasant unconcern.

These enthusiasts don't need grand preparations. For them, a little sport activity two or three times a week even for just an hour should be enough, allowing ample time for the skier's other duties. Preparation of this type is useful for those who want to dedicate themselves to cross-country skiing, but in truth, it is also for those who do downhill. The serious competitive athlete, on the other hand, needs training that takes days, months, years, and even then is not sufficient. The details of this preparation are in a later chapter. First, we will deal with the training schedule itself.

The first steps serve to accustom you to the use of the skis and poles and to get you to move yourself with them in the most natural manner possible. The substance of this discipline is to take advantage of the gliding of the skis in order to advance, gaining speed with each step and each push, whether on flat terrain, rising slopes, or in descent.

Some new skiers, like the person who is musical and "has rhythm in his blood," quickly succeed in finding the precise rhythm: then he experiences the same intoxication as the downhill skier who descends in wide curves down a mountainside covered with fresh snow.

THE TEACHING PLAN

Under the direction of a trainer, anyone can follow the well-ordered plan for cross-country. Although of large scope, it can serve equally well for champions and for those who haven't yet begun to ski.

The plan is divided into five parts:

(A) *Skiing on flat ground:* This part deals with the basic techniques of cross-country.

(Above) This is the type of long, level course on which to start a season's training. (Below) After you have achieved a certain stability, shift your training to a more varied course with straight runs, wide and narrow curves, and ascending and descending stretches.

(B) *Skiing up a slope:* The technique for ascending is basically the same as that used on flat terrain but with some variations and with something added for the steeper inclines where it isn't possible just to ski along. Ascending is also very much tied in with the kind of wax chosen which is discussed in the appropriate chapter.

(C) *Skiing down a slope:* The technique used in descent is, for the most part, the same as taught in a school for downhill skiing, taking into account that you use much lighter skis and bindings and shoes of a different type.

(D) *Skiing on courses over varying terrain:* In this part is the method for training on short courses using and combining the techniques you have learned previously.

(E) *Further preparation:* This is the type of training to carry out after having mastered the technical aspects.

SKIING ON FLAT GROUND

These exercises must be done on flat ground, in a meadow, for example, or on a frozen lake covered with a layer of snow to prevent the surface of the skis from being scratched by the ice. For novices, lay out an oval or rectangular course of not more than 200 metres (about $\frac{1}{8}$ mile) long. For more experienced students, a larger course up to 400 metres (about $\frac{1}{4}$ mile) long is possible.

On this training course, the student will learn to do the following exercises:

(1) striding without poles; striding with poles
(2) diagonal stride
(3) Finnish stride
(4) triple stride
(5) double poling
(6) double poling with one stride
(7) double poling with several strides
(8) doing turns on flat ground
(9) taking advantage of the slope of the terrain

When the student has mastered all of these exercises, he is already well on his way to becoming an accomplished cross-country skier. The exercises must be carried out with as much ease and stability as possible. Ease and stability—two fundamentals for this type of skiing.

Skiing without poles is a valuable exercise. The true function of your poles is to increase your speed, not to keep you from falling.

SKIING WITHOUT POLES

This exercise serves above all to teach stability and balance on skis, without supporting yourself on poles. The beginner is inclined to lean on the poles, spreading his arms out like a cross from fear of falling and he loses the benefit of the true function of the poles, that of helping to increase his speed.

A champion cannot waste energy in keeping his balance: all of his strength must be used to advance along the race course. If he leans on the poles too much in order to keep from falling, he loses the necessary rhythm.

The exercise of skiing without poles is accomplished by giving yourself a push or "kick" with one leg while putting the entire weight of your body on the other ski which is sliding ahead. You must bend your knees as part of this movement. At the moment of the push, your foot must be completely flat on the ski. The movement comes mainly from the bending of the knees and from the hips; the motion of the knee must be fast but smooth. When the first pushing movement is finished, the ski remaining behind is pushed ahead, sliding on the track, with none of your weight resting on it. This will advance it a little ahead of the ski that you moved previously. You must simultaneously start a new pushing movement with your other leg. The upper part of your body must be leaning forward, in a comfortable position: this is a position that each cross-country skier must naturally discover for himself in a way that responds to the requirements of movement. The arms swing alternately and without effort, slightly centered, completing the forward movement.

To find the proper rhythm of the movements, each push must be started before the start of the slowing-down phase of the preceding push. The length of the glide varies for each individual and depends on how soon this slowing down occurs.

Most common errors

Beginners, to keep their balance, don't carry all their weight on the ski that is pushed ahead, and they don't, therefore, leave the other ski completely free of weight while bringing it forward again. If the beginner doesn't carry all of his weight on the ski projected forward, his weight

You must avoid holding your arms out away from your body or leaning on your poles, both common errors that waste energy and break the rhythm of your stride.

The errors demonstrated here are bending the body too far forward and carrying the pushing leg too high at the end of the thrust.

remains partly on the back ski so his glides are shorter and the skier isn't able to develop all the muscular force that gives proper rhythm to the strides. The movements then lack fluidity; the hips are not even able to start their work. The skier in this manner cannot employ all of his muscular power but tires himself out just the same. Some skiers lift up the pushing ski an exaggerated amount, a useless and counter-productive effort. After the push, the leg should follow through a natural motion to return the ski automatically to the right position for the next push.

When you as a student have begun to find the desired stability while proceeding without ski-poles along the course deliberately prepared for beginners, you can extend your training to a different, longer run of between 500 and 800 metres (about $\frac{1}{3}$ to $\frac{1}{2}$ mile). This run should be appropriately prepared so that it presents not only some straight sections but also some curves. Some of these curves can be wide tracks, others much narrower and following closely upon each other. It is good also to lay out this course on varied terrain, but not so difficult as to require the use of poles in order to be able to move ahead. With many curves this search for balance becomes more compelling.

SKIING WITH POLES: DIAGONAL STRIDE

When you, as a student, have gained enough steadiness and proper rhythm skiing without poles, you can start to learn the diagonal stride, the stride most commonly used with poles. The energy that you use to carry your body ahead in the diagonal stride is the same as you use in the push necessary to walk, to run on foot or to ski without poles. But in the diagonal stride there is also another push—that which the opposite arm gives at the same time by pushing with the pole. Opposite arms and legs work alternately in pairs. Each push with a leg corresponds to a push with the opposite arm. From this motion comes the name "diagonal" or "alternate" stride.

The work that your legs do is the same as already seen for skiing without poles. We must now consider the work that must be done by your arms. The pole on your arm that gives the push must touch the snow with its tip lined up with the front of the opposite foot, which is also for pushing. If your left leg is the one that is giving the push, the pole in your right hand must touch the snow on a line with the tip of your left foot and vice versa. The pole should not touch the snow very far from the track of the

This is the diagonal stride, the basic movement of cross-country skiing. You push off alternately with opposing arms and legs—left leg and right arm, then right leg and left arm. You should plant the tip of your poles in the snow at a point level with the opposite foot, with the pole itself inclined slightly forward (see diagram below).

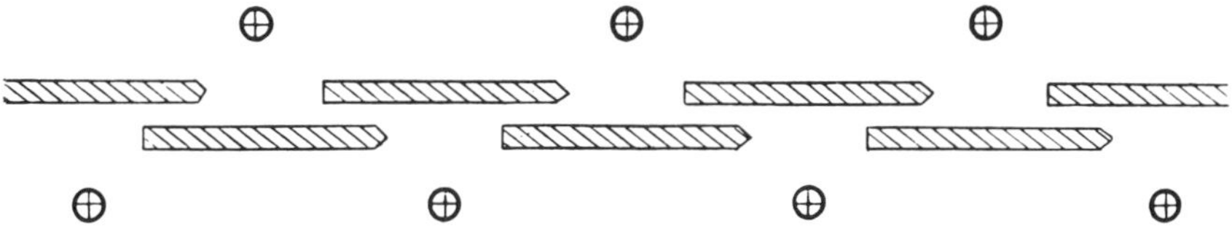

ski because in that case the energy for the push is expended first in an arc, that which your hand makes in bringing the pole back near your body, and only then is extended in the direction you want to go. Instead, the pole must be planted close to the edge of the ski in order to utilize all the energy for pushing ahead.

The pole must touch the snow in a vertical position or slightly slanted, with the handle forward. At the start, the position of your arm is slightly bent. Then your arm pulls your body toward the pole. At the same time, your hand completes a semicircle moving next to your hip, which also serves to move your body ahead. The movement continues with a further backward push with the pole which continues until your arm is behind you. To arrive at this position, your hand must be opened so that the palm faces up while still holding the handle of the pole between the thumb and index finger. The strap on the handle keeps you from losing the pole. The strap must be put on in the right way, by putting your whole hand through the circle from the bottom and grasping the strap itself as well as the pole just as in downhill skiing.

The motion of your arm, as already explained, is divided in two parts: the first part during which it pulls and the second part during which it pushes. The second part is the more important because it aids most in building up speed. The final push of the arm must be given simultaneously with the kick of the opposite leg.

The arm and the pole are brought forward again in the most natural way. Just as when skiing without poles, your arm is carried ahead bent and slightly toward center.

Most common errors in the diagonal stride

New skiers often plant their poles in the snow along a line that is too far from the tracks of the skis.

Beginners also tend to conclude the first part of the arm movement stopping the hand at the hip, but not affecting the next push, which is the most important part. When the skier doesn't open his hand near the end of the push, the push becomes too short and the pole is pulled from the snow, using the muscles uselessly.

FINNISH STRIDE

This type of movement is made up of two diagonal strides followed by another two strides, during which you straighten up your torso a little. You move the poles out in front of your body, then allow them to swing back but hold them high enough so they don't actually touch the snow.

Use the so-called Finnish stride to rest your muscles from the diagonal stride. Make two diagonal strides, then take two more strides during which you raise your body a little and let your poles swing in front of you without planting them in the snow or pushing against them. Follow this with two diagonal strides, then switch again.

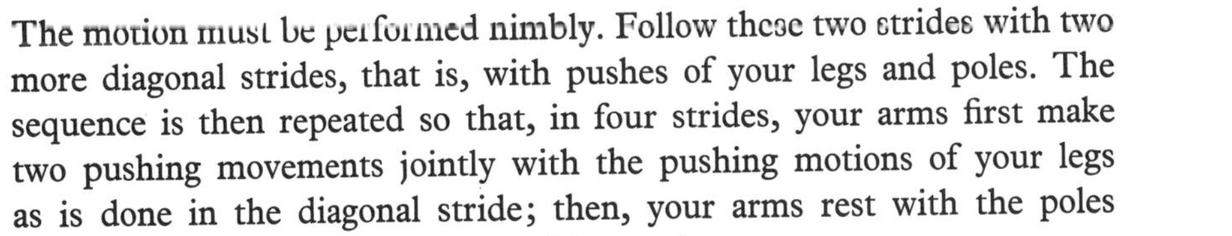

The motion must be performed nimbly. Follow these two strides with two more diagonal strides, that is, with pushes of your legs and poles. The sequence is then repeated so that, in four strides, your arms first make two pushing movements jointly with the pushing motions of your legs as is done in the diagonal stride; then, your arms rest with the poles hanging in front, ready to start pushing again.

At this point, you will want to know when you should use the diagonal

These front views of skiers using the Finnish stride show how the poles swing loosely in front of the body during alternate pairs of strides.

stride and when you should use the Finnish stride instead. Earlier we said that the diagonal stride is the most commonly used. Used too much, however, the diagonal stride tires the muscles that are employed. Even for a champion, the torso-forward position of the diagonal stride is tiring.

Very tiring, too, is all the work your arms must do with each stride. So when the muscles start to get tired while using the diagonal stride, it is a relief to straighten up for a second and to let the poles swing without using your arms.

The use of a particular stride also depends on the conditions of the terrain and on the type of snow. In general, when the snow on the course is well packed and the poles can bite in solidly, the diagonal stride will be best. When the course is not much travelled and there is such deep snow that the poles sink into the track, the diagonal stride is not advisable. Instead, it is opportune to use the Finnish stride that in effect cuts the work of the arms in half.

Most common errors in the Finnish stride

If you don't straighten up after the two diagonal strides but stay bent over during the next two strides, you won't loosen up your muscles and rest them enough. You won't even be able to swing the poles in front properly either.

Beginners are inclined to do the Finnish stride with nervous, unsmooth motions which cause them to lose the desired rhythm.

TRIPLE STRIDE

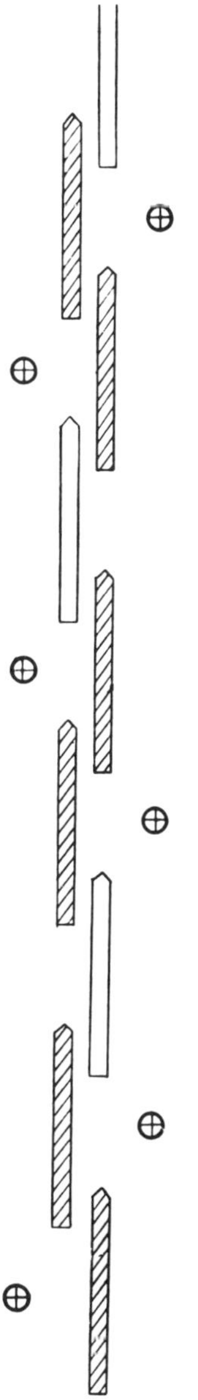

The triple stride can be used as a rest from the diagonal stride or you may be forced to use it on a course through a woods where the path is too narrow to permit you to plant your pole alongside the track. In this movement, every third stride is made without an accompanying pole thrust but you must let the pole swing out in front of you without touching the snow in order to maintain your rhythm.

A good skier must be able to change his stride to adapt it to the kind of terrain and to the type of snow as well as to give his muscles a chance to rest after prolonged effort. Changing of the stride when necessary must be accomplished spontaneously. If the course follows an extremely varied path, as when you are in a forest, it sometimes happens that you aren't able to work with one of the poles, and it swings without being used to push. This motion has already been described for the Finnish stride in which, however, both poles swing without being used. When it happens that one pole isn't being used to push, you have the triple stride. This stride is defined as a succession of diagonal strides in which every third stride is made without the push of a pole.

The triple stride is needed sometimes when you are forced to use the same pole consecutively so as not to lose your balance. The technical details of the execution of this triple stride are the same as for the diagonal and Finnish strides. The biggest difficulty in doing the triple stride is in finding the right rhythm. The novice will acquire this rhythm easily when he has begun to make some progress and skis on increasingly difficult courses. To become a good cross-country skier it is not always enough just to have the rhythm of the various strides—you must understand well what you are doing.

DOUBLE POLING

This is a technique for use on fast snow or over a descending course. Your feet move ahead side by side without pushing. With your body in an upright position, stretch your arms forward in a slightly bent position, swing the poles forward, plant them into the snow in an inclined position with the points forward in respect to the hands which hold them. The skis and body will be moving forward as a result of the push from the preceding stride or the momentum of a descending course. As your body moves forward, the poles will begin to straighten up and, at this point, bend your torso forward, applying all your weight and the strength of your arms on the poles. This downward pressure will give you a new push ahead. In this push, the hands that hold the poles move through an arc carrying them from chest height to the level of your hips, giving the push we have seen before for the other strides. Both arms must end up behind you. During the push bend your elbows, but not more than 90°.

Most common mistakes in double poling

The beginner often does not carry the torso far enough forward during the pushing phase, but keeps an upright position and does the pushing motion with straight arms, uselessly wasting a lot of energy.

Some skiers bend their elbows too much, others too little.

The arms should not stop their pushing motion at hip level, but should continue on back until the end of the movement.

On fast snow, especially over slightly descending terrain, you can use pole thrusts without strides to propel yourself forward. Both poles are planted at the same time and you use the forward thrust of your body as well as your arms to push against your poles, which then swing up behind you at the end of the movement.

DOUBLE POLING WITH ONE STRIDE

Double poling with a stride is used for the very same type of snow and terrain as double poling without a stride but when, perhaps because of a sudden change in the snow conditions, the normal double poling becomes too fatiguing. In one out of two runs, for example, you are likely to use double poling with one stride because it helps you develop more speed than ordinary double poling.

When your feet are side by side and the skis are parallel, raise your body as in the preparation for double poling. At the same time, make ready your arms to begin the work of pushing just as for double poling. At the same moment you start pushing with your arms, you also push or "kick" with one leg. The leg that does the pushing then returns immediately after into position alongside the other which has glided ahead. The skis continue to glide along parallel to one another when the

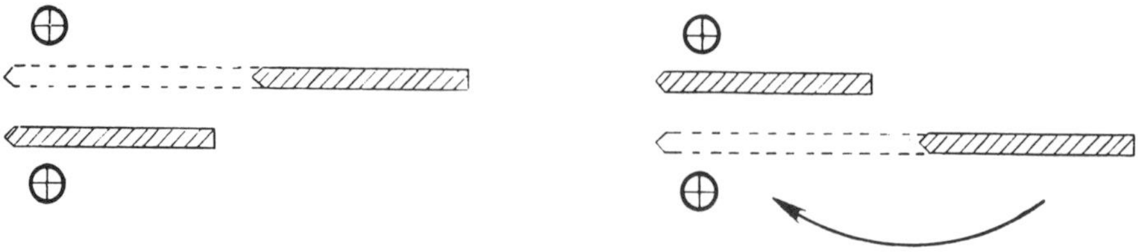

Double poling with one stride.

Sixten Jernberg of Sweden, winner of two Olympic titles and two world titles in the 50 km. (31 mi.) distance.

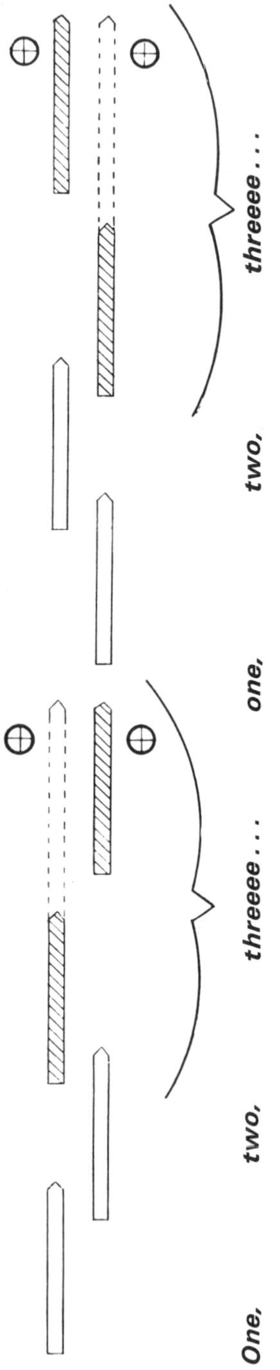
One,
two,
threeee . . .
one,
two,
threeee . . .

pushing movement is finished. There is no exact rule about which leg to use for the push. You can use either one or alternate them but if one of your legs is stronger than the other, there should be no doubt about your choice.

You may choose to use double poling with one stride when you begin to tire from using double poling. Double poling with one stride requires, in fact, a movement that takes better advantage of the forward thrust of the body and the muscles. The particulars of the movement are the same as those used for double poling.

DOUBLE POLING WITH SEVERAL STRIDES

The Nordic-style skier, after having gone a distance using the diagonal stride or the Finnish stride may start to feel tired legs and the desire to rest them. In case this happens to you, you can use double poling in a cycle following a set number of strides without it. This allows you to work less with your legs while requiring a greater contribution from your arm and torso muscles. Usually the double-poling push is given with every three strides, but in some cases may be given with every four or five strides.

The push every three strides is executed by raising your torso and effecting two faster and shorter strides than in the diagonal stride. During these strides, bring the ski poles into position to effect the double-pole push as in double poling with one stride. The push is done on the third stride exactly as in the case of double poling with one stride. Translated into words, the rhythm of this stride assumes the following tone: one, two, threeeee . . . one, two, threeeee . . .

TURNING ON FLAT GROUND

Every cross-country skier is going to find himself faced with the need to turn both on slopes and on flat ground.

(Opposite) Walter Demel of Germany, a leading contender in the 15-km. and 30-km. distances. After going a distance with the diagonal stride that Demel is using here, you can switch to double poling in a cycle following a fixed number of strides taken without planting your poles. The movement and rhythm for double poling with every third stride is shown in the diagram.

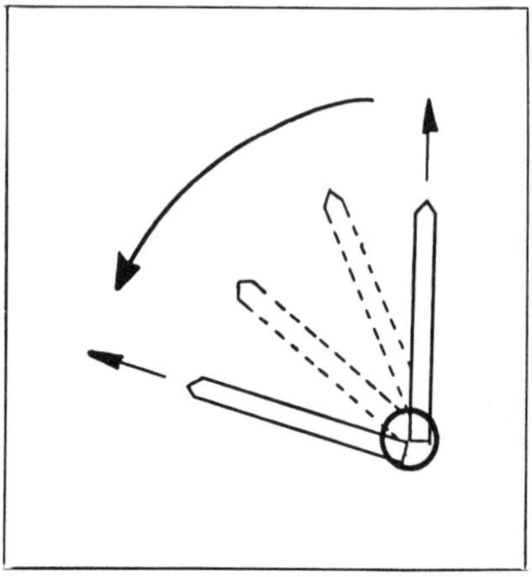

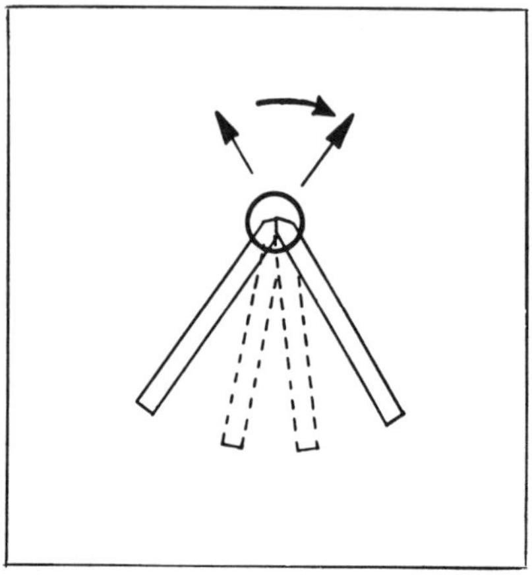

(Left) The easiest way to turn is to shift one ski in the new direction by raising the tip and pivoting on the tail. Bring the other ski alongside and repeat the movement. (Right) You can also turn by pivoting on the tip and raising the tail but this is a less natural movement and requires more experience.

The easiest way to change directions on flat terrain is to first shift the left ski (if you want to turn to the left) towards the new direction, and then bring the other ski back alongside it. Continue this series of two movements until you are headed in the new direction. The movement is accomplished by raising the tip of the ski and pivoting on the snow with the tail end. It is also possible to turn by pivoting on the tip and raising the tail, but the movement is less natural and requires more skiing experience. During races the movement will naturally be more complex,

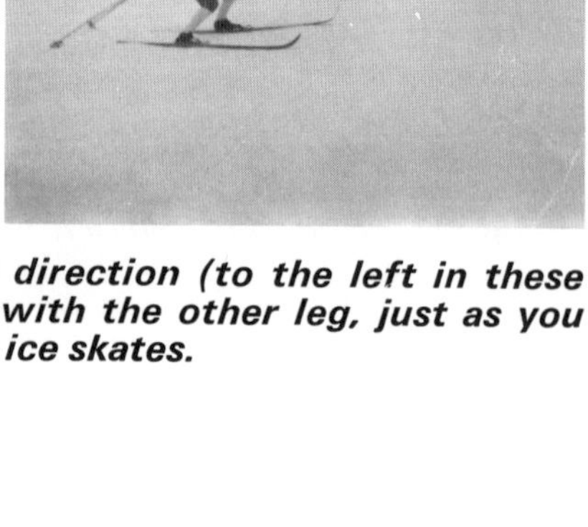

As one ski is turned in the new direction (to the left in these photos), give an energetic push with the other leg, just as you would do on ice skates.

After giving a push with the opposite leg, shift your weight back to the turned ski, gliding forward on it as you move the other ski back alongside. Use your poles to push as in double poling without strides.

because while you are turning, it is often possible with practiced technique to increase your speed or at least not diminish it.

It is most important to learn to turn well, because nowadays the courses over which races are run have many turns even on the flat part of the track.

TURNS ON OPEN GROUND

During races, a turn is made by shifting one ski towards the new direction while the other leg gives a strong push like that used in skating. Using the example of a left turn, at the same moment that you initiate the turning movement, you must bend your knees while shifting the weight of your body onto your right leg. With this leg you give a sideways and forward push. While executing the push, the tip of the left ski must be raised toward the new direction. When the weight of your body shifts to your left leg, your left ski glides ahead. The right ski is automatically drawn back in place alongside the left and a new turning-pushing movement can begin. These movements continue in succession until you are headed in the desired direction. To turn to the right, you have to carry out the same movements, but now the left leg does the pushing and the right ski glides ahead. The poles help with the movement as they do in double poling, and the arms do their pushing simultaneously with the push of the leg.

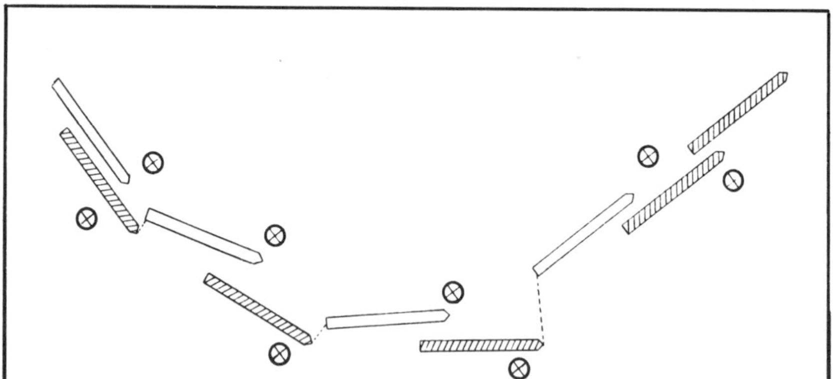

Franco Nones, competing in the 1968 Olympics 30-km. race, makes a perfect turn to the right. In racing, you must maintain both your speed and your rhythm as you turn, for it is often the stretches of track with the most turns that determine the outcome of a race.

Your balance must be perfect and you must not fail to shift all your weight onto the ski that is gliding ahead once the other leg has given its push.

TURNS IN THE WOODS

In the woods, due to plants and other obstacles close to the track, turning can be perilous since the ski that gives the push, in the movement of returning to place, can bump against something and break, or cause a

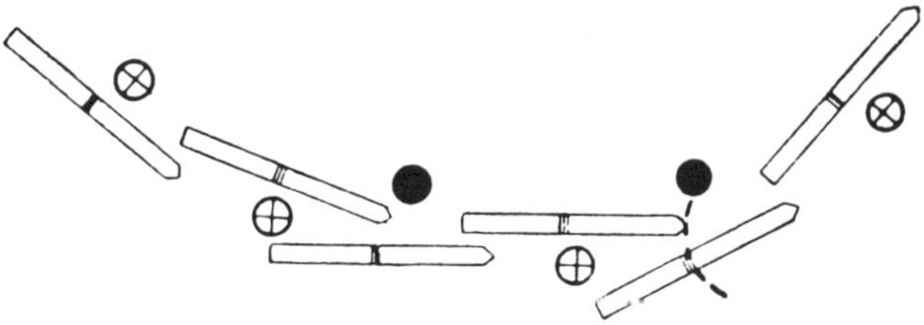

Turning in the woods requires that you keep the tips of your skis under perfect control. Move the outside ski forward in the new direction with its inside edge resting lightly on the snow, the outside edge slightly raised. When your outside foot is level with the tip of your inside ski, shift your weight to the outside ski. Then move the inside ski alongside. Use your inside pole (the black dot in the diagram) as a support.

ruinous fall. It is important to constantly check the position of the tips of the skis and, therefore, it is advisable to turn with a different type of diagonal stride.

Move the outside ski ahead and "plant" it in the snow in such a way that the tip is pointed towards the new direction and the outside edge is slightly raised. The foot on the outside ski should be opposite the tip of the inside ski. The movement that carries the outside ski ahead is made so that the weight of your body shifts to that ski which then rests completely on the snow. Now bring the inside ski on which the push was given, up alongside the outside ski as in the normal diagonal stride. At this point, give the outside leg a push to send the inside ski ahead, as in the diagonal stride. Continue this alternating motion until the skis are pointed in the desired direction. Bear in mind that the legs furnish the push for this turn, just as in the diagonal stride, and the skis should never stop moving, particularly the outside one, but continue to glide along the entire arc of the turn.

Your body, in executing turns, must be leaning slightly forward. The poles work as in the diagonal stride, but the inside one, besides pushing, must also serve for support. In fact, during the turn, the weight of the body tends to throw a skier off balance forward and towards the inside.

A competitor, especially, should learn the technique for turning on flat terrain. Many times during a race it is precisely the stretch of the course with the most turns that determines the victory of one athlete over another, since it is turning that requires the greatest technical capability.

When a skier does not have good technique in turning, he makes the turn simply by strength, wasting his energy uselessly. It is like a fighter in a boxing match—a bad turn isn't a knock-out punch, but it is the first of a series of blows that in a short time can put you out of the fight.

It is, therefore, indispensable to learn thoroughly all the systems for turning, and it is also necessary to know in which case to use one rather than another.

Most common errors in executing turns

The loss of stability is the most common. The skier is afraid to shift all of his weight onto the gliding ski and in the process of returning the leg that gave the push, he puts his weight back too quickly on both skis, losing the proper rhythm of the movement. He also loses the rhythm of the course. A cross-country course, like the special slalom course, has its own rhythm. If a skier loses the rhythm of the course, the tips of his skis can go over into fresh snow, throwing him off the track at the cost of precious time and energy.

TAKING ADVANTAGE OF THE SLOPE OF THE TERRAIN

People talk about the necessity of finding the rhythm of the movements. The more a skier knows about the technique of the strides, the easier it will be to find this rhythm.

They also talk about the rhythm of the course. A course for cross-country skiing is not a lifeless thing, made of straight, smooth tracks along which the skier can run like a robot. A course is, instead, more like the bed of a brook and your skis have to run along it just as the water does.

Due to some sinking of the snow, a course when it is laid out will likely include some hollows that are more or less deep and wide, small humps and some actual holes. A skier must know the best way to approach these irregularities. A skier's movements must harmonize with the rhythm of the course. You must not approach these uneven patches with your body rigid because that is tiring and will cause you to lose time. Moreover, you run the risk of breaking a ski. If, on the contrary, your motions are loose and agile, these unequal parts of the course can be used to increase your speed.

If you are skiing along using the diagonal stride, for example, you can take advantage of a slight hollow to get a stronger push. If you can manage to give the kick just as your foot is above the hollow, the ski will act like a spring. Naturally, this push must be carefully controlled or you risk breaking a ski when the hollow is very deep.

If you are skiing along a bumpy track and manage to give a push with one ski while it is at the bottom of a gully, the other ski will have to go up a rise. This mound should be surmounted with ease thanks to the extra push

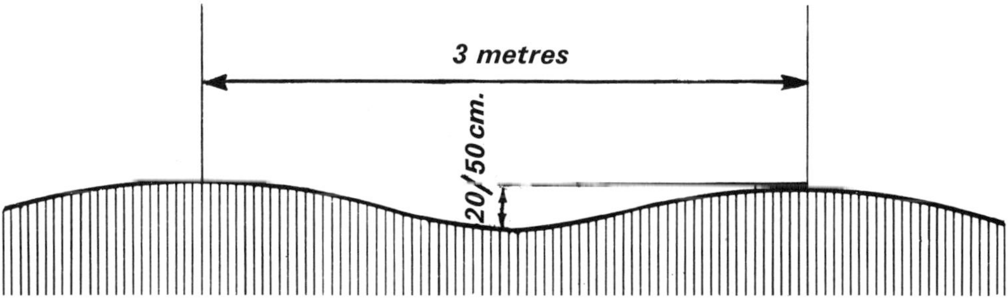

An experienced skier can take advantage of rises and hollows in the track to increase his speed. If you lay out a training course, make the rises 3 metres (about 10 feet) apart and 20 to 50 centimetres (8 to 20 inches) high.

of the preceding kick, and the following push can perhaps be given when the ski reaches the next hollow.

If instead, you arrive at the top of a mound with your skis side by side and the hollow dipping down ahead is quite deep, it is better to push with the skis just as soon as the rise is surmounted so as to build up impetus for the rise that follows.

These notions will be more comprehensible when you study them directly with skis on your feet over a rolling terrain. This being the case, it is possible to lay out your own teaching course, using a shovel to create hollows and mounds. Make the length of each hollow $1\frac{1}{2}$ times that of a ski and vary the depth from 8 to 20 inches (20–50 cm.).

You can also build a length of teaching course in which a hollow in the track for one ski corresponds to a bump in the track for the other. In this case, the length of the hollows should be about 2 yards (2 metres), the length of a ski with the depth the same as above. On this type of run you ski using the diagonal stride with more rapid movements. The foot starts to press against the ski as soon as it is over the rise and the pushing movement is completed when the ski gets to the very bottom of the hollow. In Sweden, this last type of run is called an "organ pedal" course. Using the proper technique, it is even possible to increase your speed by taking advantage of these depressions in the track.

SKIING UP A SLOPE

Laymen probably do not realize that you can also ski up a slope. Those who don't know modern cross-country technique may believe that to go up a slope on the snow they must put sealskin under their skis like the old Norsemen did. In a cross-country race, therefore, they may find going uphill difficult even though in men's competition the course may rise or fall as much as 820 feet (250 metres).

Naturally, you don't have time to put sealskin under the skis during competition and this is where the proper use of wax becomes important. Like a downhill skier, a cross-country skier must wax his skis according to the kind of snow on the course. But the downhill skier needs to think only about going down fast: the cross-country skier, on the other hand, must also have in addition a type of wax that keeps the skis from sliding backwards when giving the push for the different strides and for when he must ascend a slope.

Special waxes are now produced for about ten different types of snow.

These waxes can also be combined so it is possible to find the proper type of waxing for all the kinds of snow that nature offers. To avoid mistakes in waxing, an athlete needs long practical experience, and his preparation must be meticulous each time. A beginner, therefore, must reconcile himself to carefully reading the instructions written on the tubes of wax.

Wax is an important factor, but to ski up a slope it is also necessary to know the technique to use. For ascending, the strides to use are the diagonal, the triple, and the Finnish, naturally with some variations. The diagonal stride is used most often. Double poling or double poling with one stride aren't ordinarily used.

Going uphill is tiring, so it is important not to waste energy using the muscles more than necessary. The rhythm of the movements should be the same as on flat ground. In the diagonal, triple, and Finnish stride used for ascending, both the stride and the glide of the ski are naturally shorter than on flat ground.

For the strides used for ascending, the ski poles should be stuck into the snow sooner than on flat ground, and your arms should start their

In a cross-country race, you may encounter some difficult ascents. You must adjust your strides by making them shorter and by planting your poles sooner.

work before the opposite leg starts pushing, in order to avoid sliding backwards. Your arms should be bent so as to form a smaller angle between the biceps and forearms than that formed for the push with strides done on flat ground. The poles should be held with the handle towards the middle of your body. The muscles work more efficiently this way. Your torso should not be held too far forward and your hips not moved too far behind. The knees are bent forward more than on flat ground, a position which allows a more efficient push and doesn't make you slide backwards.

To give the muscles a rest, competitors always ski loosely with short strides, especially for short, steep inclines. This way they use some muscles other than those normally used. The position of your body should be more erect.

For very steep inclines, you must use other methods—the herringbone, the ladder or "stair step" and the transverse ladder also known as "sidestepping."

HERRINGBONE

Spread the tips of the skis apart while keeping the tails close together. Turn your knees inward which automatically raises the outside edges of the skis.

If you go up an incline this way, follow the line of maximum slope, working the poles alternately with your steps, planting the poles into the snow behind the skis.

For very steep ascents such as you will encounter in touring, not in prepared race courses, you must use special techniques like the herringbone step.

LADDER

Also known as the lateral stair step, this is a less tiring but slower system for ascending a steep slope.

Arrange your skis parallel to one another and perpendicular to the line of the slope. Begin going up by lifting the higher ski towards the top and then drawing the lower ski up next to it. Continue this motion to the top of the slope.

During the movement your knees should be flexed toward the summit while the skis press into the snow with the edges that are toward the top of the hill. Incline your torso slightly downhill, a position that will keep you from slipping sideways.

Use this method when the slope is too steep for you to use the herringbone.

TRANSVERSE LADDER

This is a method similar to the simple ladder with the difference that the upper ski is carried ahead and to the side each time. Bring the lower ski alongside just as in the ladder step. If the slope is very long, it may be necessary to proceed along a zigzag course.

To turn while ascending, use the system described earlier for flat ground, holding the tips of the skis spread apart. It is necessary, however, to block yourself from behind with the poles to keep from sliding backwards.

These three methods of ascending are used more while touring in hills

Other techniques for ascending steep terrain are the ladder step and the transverse ladder. These are slower but less tiring than the herringbone step.

or mountains than during a race. Actual race courses generally have lengths of uphill runs that can be negotiated by skiing or by running. Sometimes though you may have to use the herringbone or transverse ladder in a race.

If, during a race, you are using the transverse ladder, you will not need to zigzag because the course will never be laid out to be long and steep at the same time.

SKIING DOWNHILL

The technique for going downhill is basically the same as is taught in schools of downhill skiing and in books that cover this material.

Since a cross-country skier follows a course made like a track, not a wide, beaten course as for downhill skiing, there are some substantial differences. This kind of course forces the skis into a mandatory position and doesn't allow you to make certain movements of control, or give you the possibility of braking.

Consider also that cross-country competition skis weigh only from 1200–1450 grams (2.65–3.2 pounds) while downhill skis vary from 5–7 kilograms (about 11–15½ pounds). On cross-country skis your feet are attached only by the edge of the tip of the shoe, while on downhill skis your feet are firmly attached.

Also, the footgear is very different: boots for cross-country are light and soft (some are made of kangaroo skin), with thinner leather than is used for walking shoes. Downhill boots, on the other hand, are very heavy and stiff.

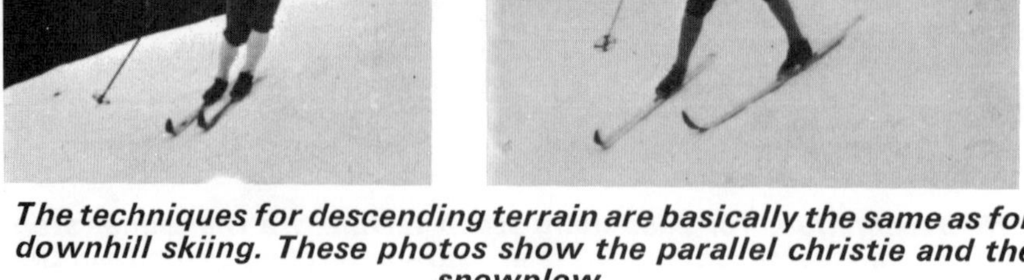

The techniques for descending terrain are basically the same as for downhill skiing. These photos show the parallel christie and the snowplow.

Lars-Göran Aslund of Sweden, winner of the 1970 15-km. World Championship, on a downhill stretch of the track.

All that aside, the modern technique for downhill skiing is a fine base for a cross-country skier. The preparers of today's courses for cross-country racing are including long, challenging downhill stretches more and more frequently in their layouts, so it is ever more necessary for a cross-country skier to be a good downhill skier also.

COURSE WITH VARIED DIFFICULTIES

A student of downhill skiing, after a little while, is annoyed performing the same exercises over and over in the school practice field and yearns to plunge down a long slope to taste the intoxication of speed. A cross-country student, also, soon wants to go out by himself on the course to experience the pleasure of going cross-country. Practicing on a short circular course over flat ground becomes tedious. To relieve the effort and to make training more interesting, the instructor can trace out a course

with varied challenges as an alternative to the flat track described at the beginning, the length varying from 400 metres to one or two kilometres (about $\frac{1}{4}$ mile to 1 mile). The course should be laid out with a succession of difficult situations to give the student a chance to apply the various techniques learned on the circular course.

The instructor should first go with the students along the course to explain how to overcome each of the difficulties and then should follow their progress from a good observation point to be able to make necessary and helpful criticism.

On these courses technique can be refined and the student will come to realize the importance of knowing all the fine details. You must learn when and why it is necessary to change strides, to follow the contour of the land, to approach turns with agility, to go up slopes conserving as much energy as possible and to descend quickly and with perfect balance.

Besides brushing up on technique, on these courses you will improve your breathing and speed. The majority of skiers, whether beginners or champions, rarely have the desire to go on with technical training. They start preparing too soon on long, hard training or competition courses. They fail to calmly acquire the necessary technique or the right rhythm. They learn to ski more by strength than with technique. The strides are done rigidly and the skier uselessly wastes a great deal of energy.

It is important that the instructor, during the first 10 or 15 days of training in the snow, present complete instruction in technique to his students. The importance of this becomes clear when actual competition begins. Note that this repetition of techniques serves not only to make beginners masters of the material, but also helps champions who already know it to find balance and rhythm.

At this same time, you should also practice on courses that are longer but easier without forcing yourself.

CONTINUING PREPARATION

After several days of perfecting technique, those who don't intend to dedicate themselves to competition can start short cross-country tours for recreation. Competition skiers should continue to follow a well defined schedule instead.

The majority of athletes are quick to overdo it and start their preparation with too much enthusiasm. The important thing at the beginning is to put distance on your feet. Every skier in training should keep a record of the distance covered every day. This "distance training" is done on laid-out courses and also on fresh snow where the distance covered should reach 25–50 km. (15–30 miles), occasionally even longer.

To find the right rhythm for your legs, start training on short, well-laid-out courses from a minimum of 2–3 km. (about $1\frac{1}{2}$ miles) to a maximum of 10–15 km. (6–9 miles). You will augment the velocity somewhat in this new phase of training. This type of training is combined with "interval training," that is, training in which you alternate 1 or 2 km. (0.6 to 1.2 miles) of fast run with 1 km. (0.6 mile) at a more tranquil pace. Ski along in this fashion until you feel sufficiently tired out. Complete your training with special preparation in ascending and descending slopes.

None of these types of training are ever stopped completely, but are resumed periodically according to the personal plan of each athlete—whatever needs to be planned to provide effective but enjoyable preparation.

During training you need to observe and deal with certain important details as, for example, getting the body used to ingesting lukewarm, sweet drinks during prolonged exertion. Your body needs these to rebuild the energy consumed during effort that might go on for two, even four, hours.

You should also test out the wax, equipment, etc.

Races begin soon, perhaps after only three weeks of training in the snow. From that moment it is necessary that the training plan fit in with the racing schedule. Maintaining the training plan is complicated by the travel necessary to reach the locations where races are held—trips to foreign countries in the case of international competition.

In this period of training and racing, the greatest difficulty for an athlete is finding time to rest. The days of rest have the same importance as the days of training and racing. Unfortunately, the days of rest are too few for full-time competitors, generally one a week.

The idea of training in technique isn't to make all skiers alike. Each one must find his own way of skiing, but all should know the basic principles of technique. The sequence drawings shown here are based on photographs of champion skiers taken during recent World Championship and Olympic competitions.

Descent is part of cross-country skiing and the technique of descent is very important. The line drawings shown here are based on photographs of champions taken during the competition at Holmenkollen in 1970 and 1971.

Speed depends very much on ski wax. Olav G. Eikrehagen (a Norwegian expert with the Oslo Institute of Physical Education) studied cross-country techniques on descending terrain with a view to discovering where and how it might be possible to gain time in a race. He came to the conclusion that the majority of skiers assume a position that is not sufficiently aerodynamic and that many are too rigid and lack stability. Considering that on most championship courses a quarter of the total time is spent on descending terrain, you can understand the importance of downhill technique. Since the total amount of time dedicated to ascending terrain, however, represents about 65 per cent of the final time, the majority of skiers train their hearts and lungs all year to be able to ski quickly uphill, completely neglecting the technique of descent.

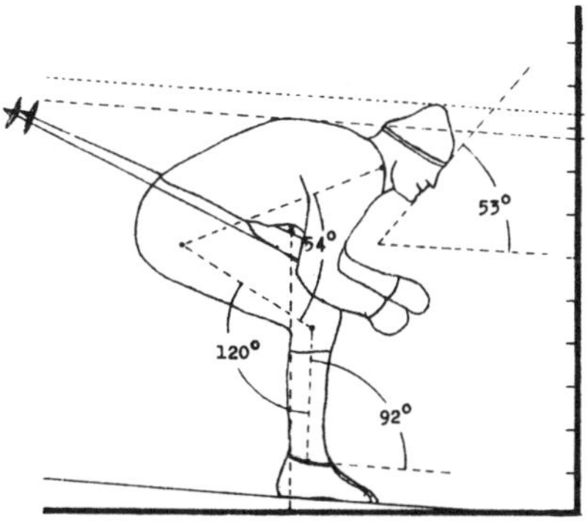

Gert-Dietmar Klaus (East Germany), weight 170 lbs. (77 kg.), height 6 ft. 2½ in. (184 cm.), speed 32.8 ft. (10.0 m.) per sec.

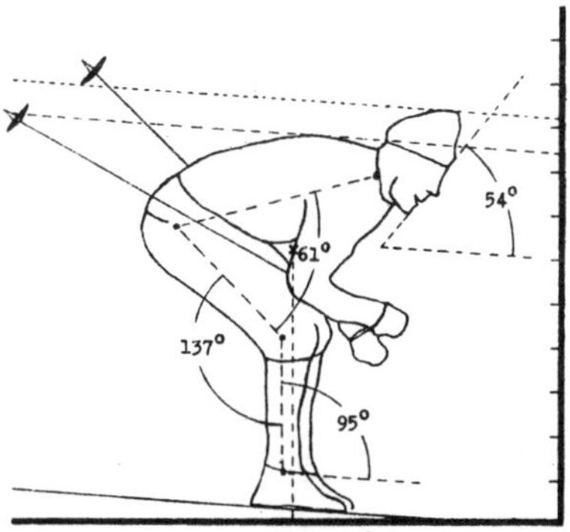

Magne Myrmo (Norway), weight 154 lbs. (70 kg.), height 5 ft. 9½ in. (177 cm.), speed 31. 5 ft. (9.6 m.) per sec.

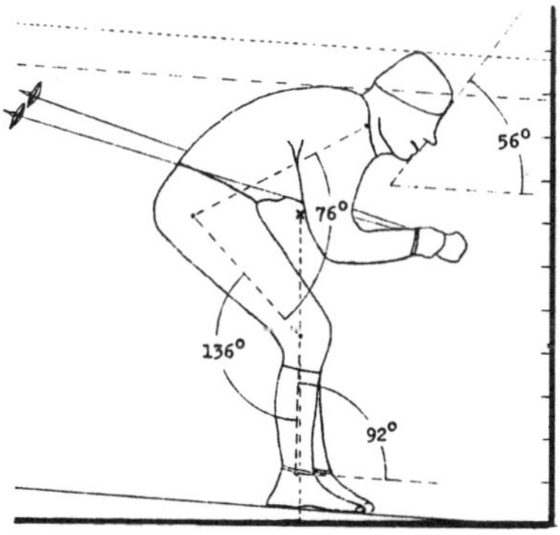

Jan Halvarsson (Sweden), weight 161 lbs. (73 kg.), height 5 ft. 11½ in. (182 cm.), speed 31.5 ft. (9.6 m.) per sec.

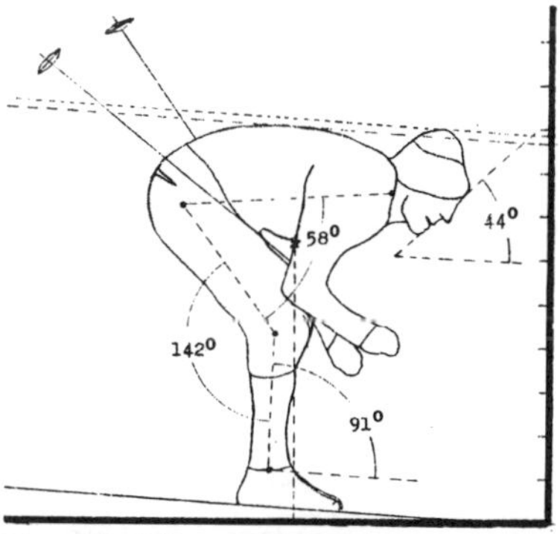

Ole Ellefsäter (Norway), weight 174 lbs. (79 kg.), height 6 ft. (183 cm.), speed 31.5 ft. (9.6 m.) per sec.

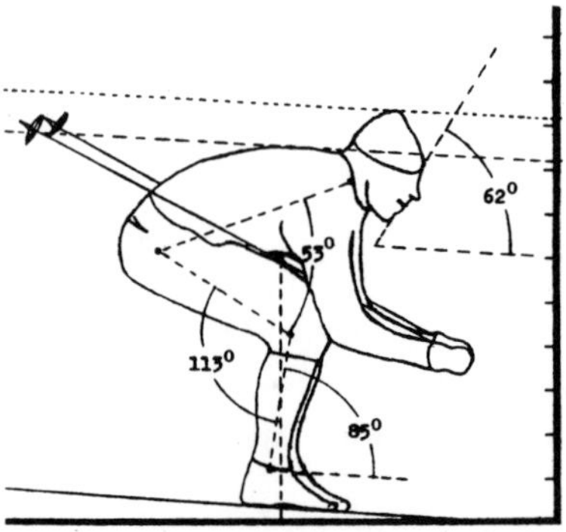

Odd Martinsen (Norway), weight 168 lbs. (76 kg.), height 6 ft. (183 cm.), speed 31.5 ft. (9.47 m.) per sec.

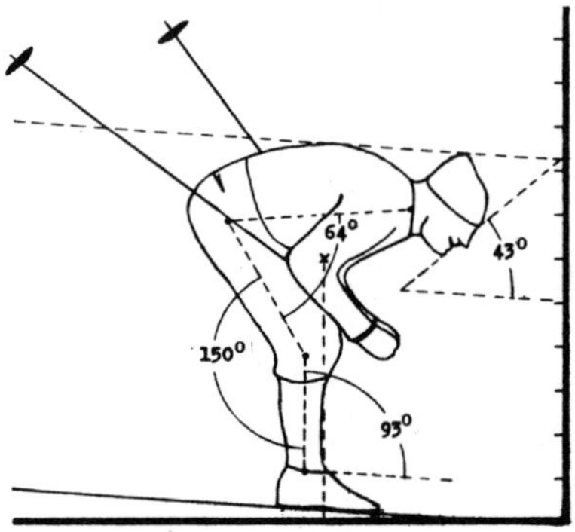

Walter Demel (East Germany), weight 146 lbs. (66 kg.), height 5 ft. 6 in. (168 cm.), speed 31.1 ft. (9.47 m.) per sec.

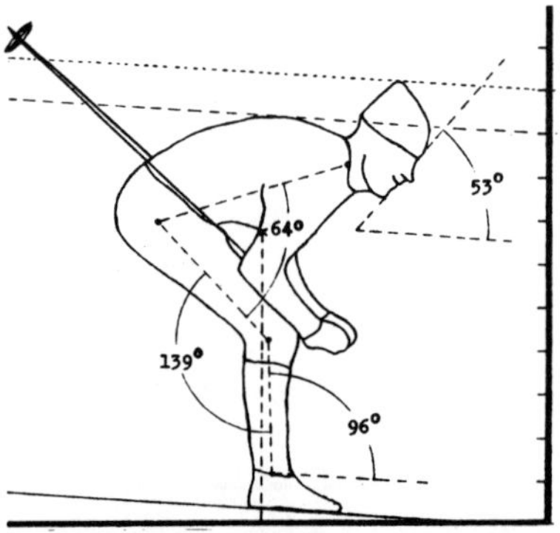

Lars-Göran Aslund (Sweden), weight 168 lbs. (76 kg.), height 6 ft. 1 in. (185 cm.), speed 31.1 ft. (9.47 m.) per sec.

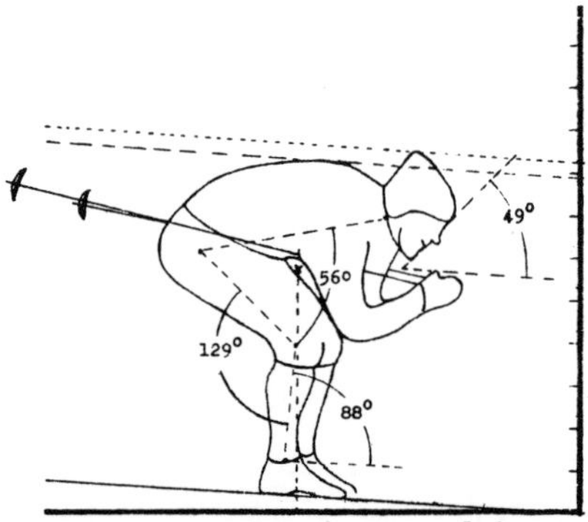

Franco Nones (Italy), weight 139 lbs. (63 kg.), height 5 ft. 6 in. (168 cm.), speed 31.1 ft. (9.47 m.) per sec.

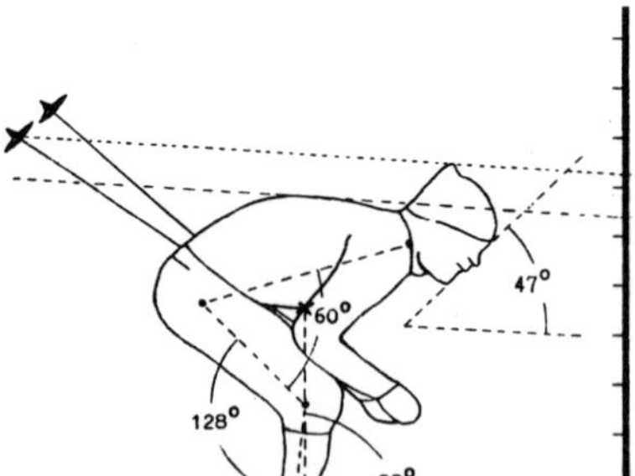

Fedor Simasov (Russia), weight 141 lbs. (64 kg.), height 5 ft. 5 in. (166 cm.), speed 30.28 ft. (9.23 m.) per sec.

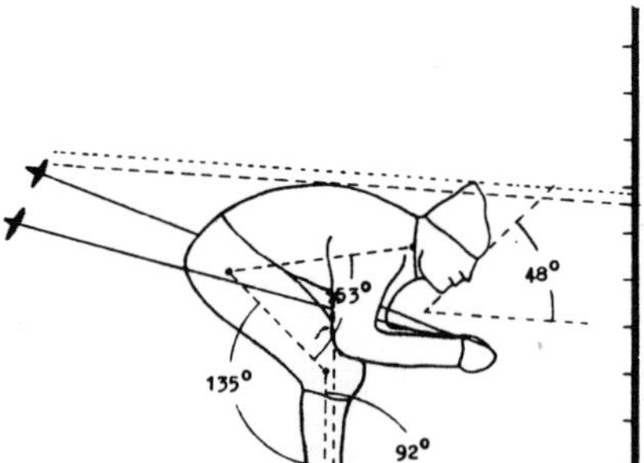

Wjaceslav Vedenin (Russia), weight 141 lbs. (64 kg.), height 5 ft. 4½ in. (164 cm.), speed 30.28 ft. (9.23 m.) per sec.

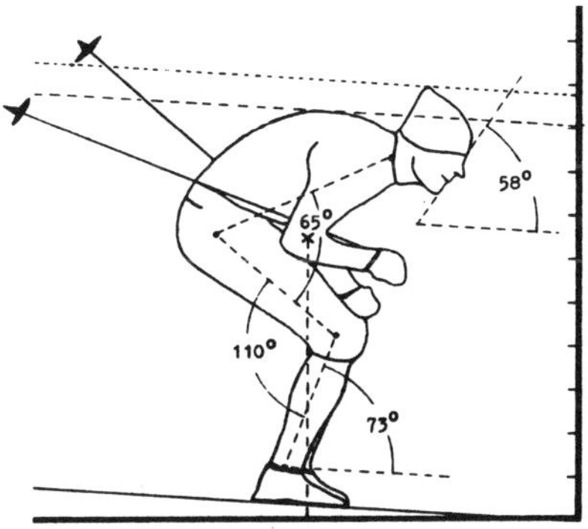

Ulrich Kostner (Italy), weight 152 lbs. (69 kg.), height 5 ft. 10½ in. (179 cm.), speed 30.28 ft. (9.23 m.) per sec.

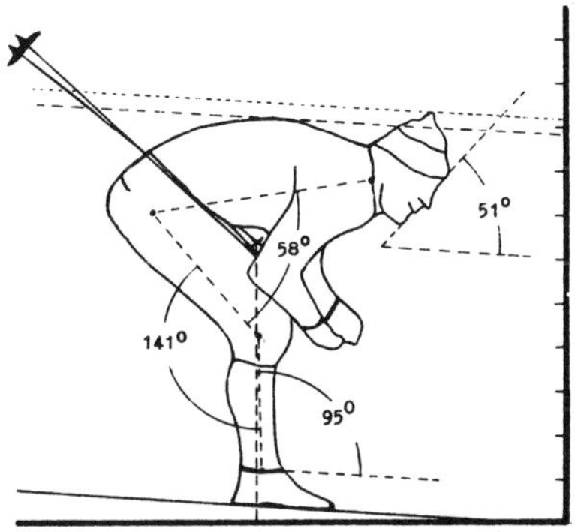

Pal Tyldum (Norway), weight 165 lbs. (75 kg.), height 5 ft. 11 in. (181 cm.), speed 29.9 ft. (9.11 m.) per sec.

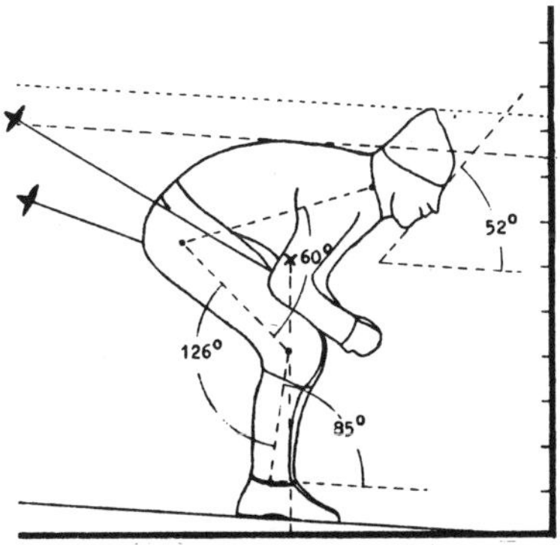

Carlo Favre (Italy), weight 168 lbs. (76 kg.), height 5 ft. 11 in. (180 cm.), speed 29.9 ft. (9.11 m.) per sec.

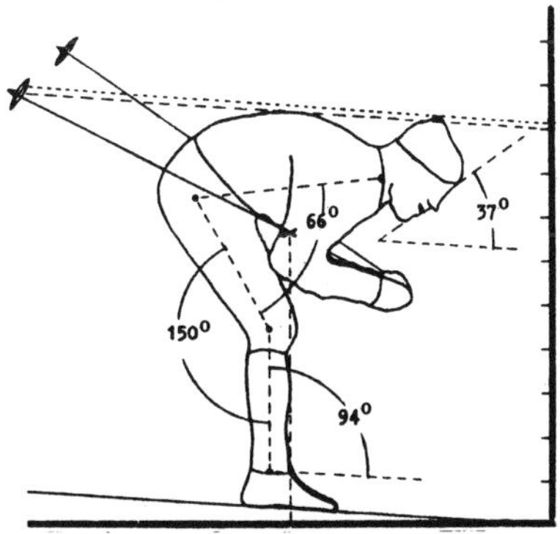

Gerhard Grimmer (East Germany), weight 150 lbs. (68 kg.), height 5 ft. 8½ in. (174 cm.), speed 29.5 ft. (8.68 m.) per sec.

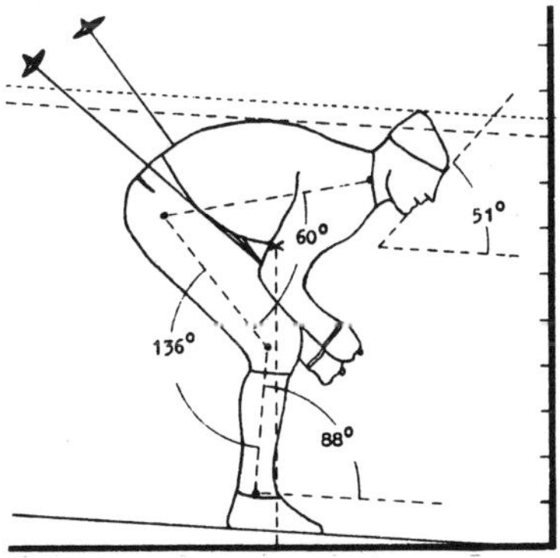

Johs Harviken (Norway), weight 163 lbs. (74 kg.), height 6 ft. 1 in. (185 cm.), speed 28.5 ft. (8.68 m.) per sec.

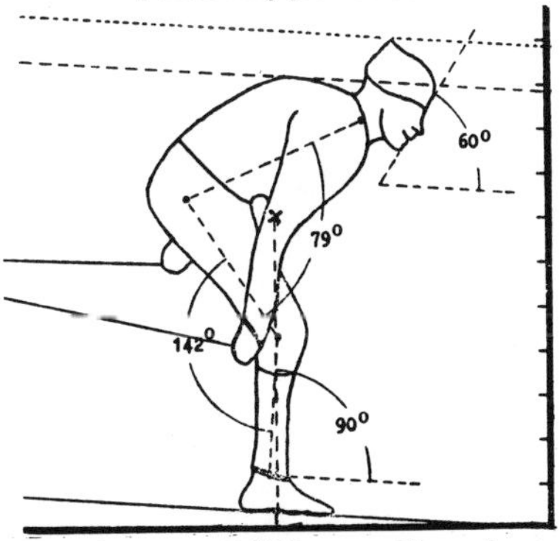

Lars-Arne Bölling (Sweden), weight 146 lbs. (66 kg.), height 5 ft. 10½ in. (179 cm.), speed 28.5 ft. (8.68 m.) per sec.

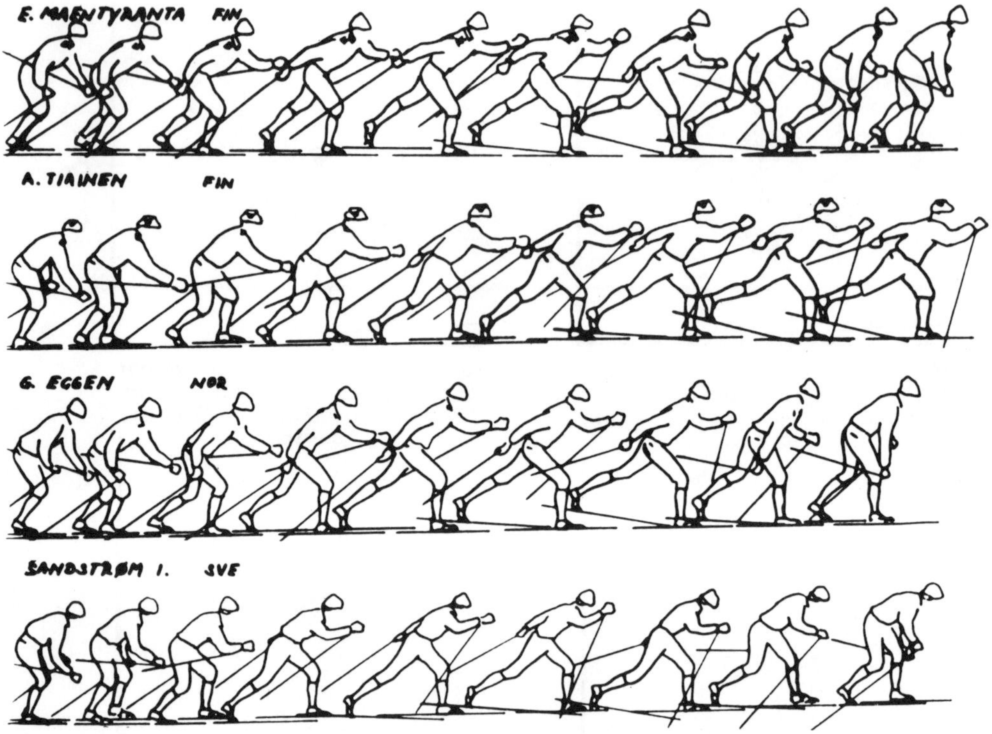

1966 World Championship

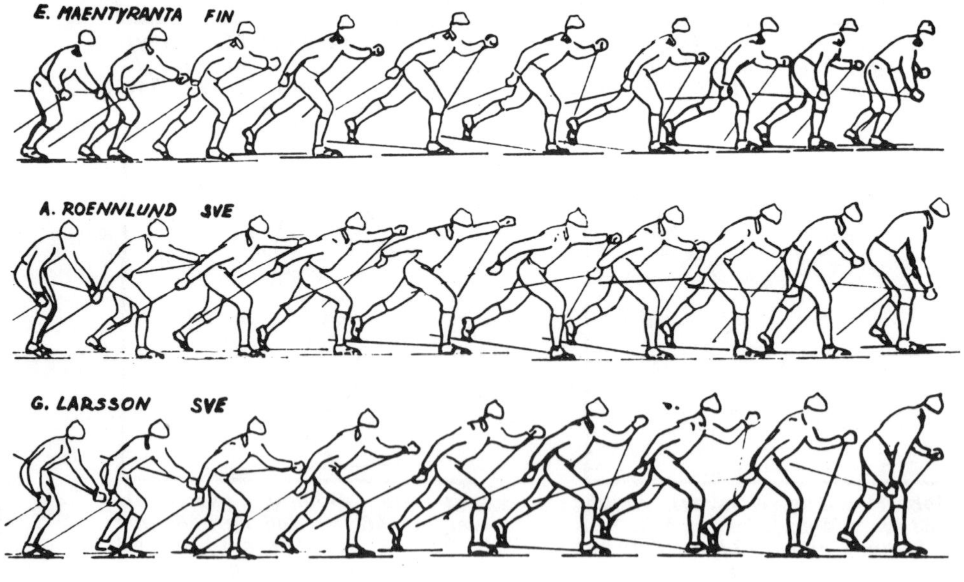

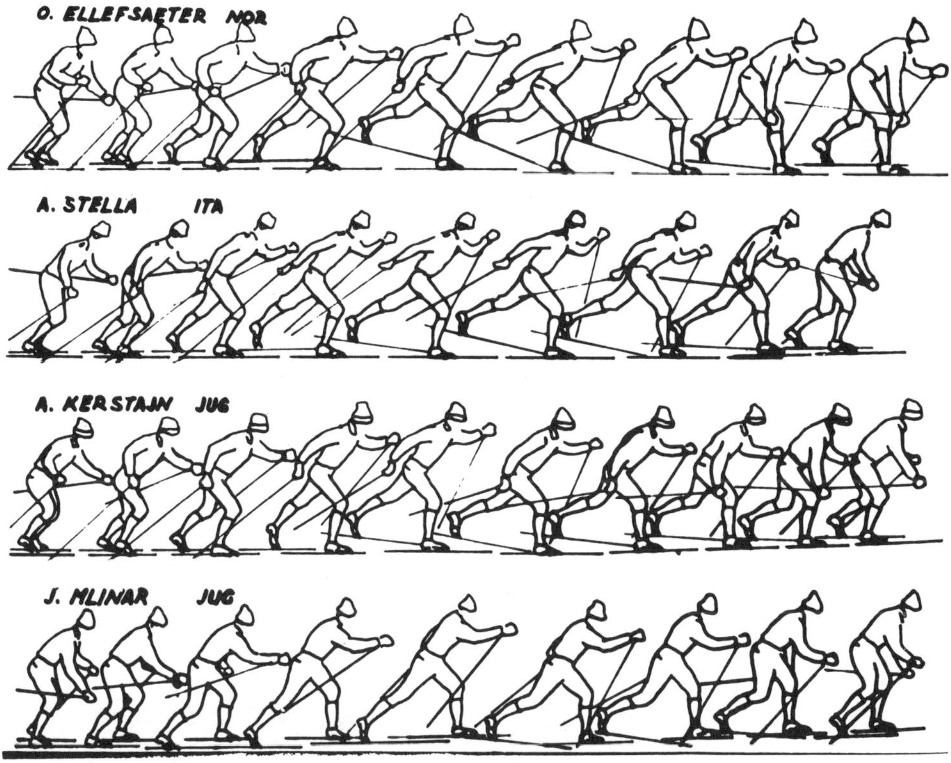

1968 Olympic Winter Games

1972 Olympic Winter Games

Contenders in international competition display a variety of styles.

Each skier in a race puts forth his best effort.

A competitive skier begins his training months before an important race.

Racing

Basically, there are no differences between the technique, the conduct of a race and the equipment for a champion and a skier who is not yet at that level. "Racing" is a word that by itself stirs interest. In it is the concept of battle. Every race has its hero, the idol of the day; these champions set an example for young skiers to follow.

For an athlete who trains so many months to attain good physical condition and perfect his technique, the race represents a goal. For the others—those who do cross-country touring, and beginning skiers—those who don't train to take part in the competition, the object is naturally different: they aim to draw satisfaction and pleasure out of the sport.

To understand all that happens before, during and after a race, you must consider the point of view of both the athletes and the trainers.

THE THREE ROUTINES—TRAINING, RACING, TRAVELLING

Races for cross-country skiers generally begin as soon as there is enough snow. Even before this, the athletes engage in time trials among themselves as "break in" exercises and to fire the competitive spirit—hoping it will continue to burn for the entire season. In these first trials on the home track, perhaps not every athlete on the team does his best, but the skiers are beginning to live in the atmosphere of competition already. From the moment the racing season starts, these trials become part of the training routine.

The travel plan must also be co-ordinated with the first two. Trips are frequently more tiring than the races, but they are inevitable for anyone who wants to compete at a high level. You must go looking for the strongest opponents where they compete. When you travel, it is difficult to arrive at your destination in perfect physical condition, but you can accustom yourself to the discomforts of this life in a way that will eliminate the negative consequences.

A Nordic skier must be not only athletically gifted, but also physically strong. A weak, sensitive type is better off staying far from obligations. A competitor may show great class on skis, but he will never be a champion unless he can stand up to the strains of training and travel as well without showing the effects of differences in climate, of different kinds of cooking, of continuously changing beds and environment, of the various means of transportation (train, plane, car) and of coming into contact with all kinds of people.

In spite of these difficulties, the athlete must follow his training routine throughout the competitive season. There may be long periods, possibly three or four weeks, during which he will compete for a distance of only 10–15 km. (6–9 miles). What would happen if an athlete suddenly found himself having to compete over long distances, not having continued his preparation?

The most difficult part of a training schedule is the inclusion of a day of rest. It is clear that the period dedicated to rest occupies only a small part in the full season's training routine, particularly when it coincides with the racing period. Nevertheless, the day of rest should absolutely be observed. When the merry-go-round of racing starts its whirl, the body and the mind of each athlete are subjected to great exertion; the constitution endures for a long while but sometimes needs a complete rest. Unfortunately, it is often inevitable that the rest day coincides with travelling, so moving from place to place should be done in the most comfortable way. As an example of the strain of a competitive season, it is sufficient to recall that some years ago in a period of three weeks during January, the Italian team raced in six different countries—Sweden, Norway, Russia, Switzerland, France and Italy. They ran as many as eight races in five of the six countries. You can see how the will power that each athlete possesses is very important.

ARRIVAL AT THE DESTINATION

On arrival at the scene of a race, you leave the train, plane, bus or whatever has brought you and you start to unload your baggage—a task that usually seems enormous. Emotion and nervousness is in the air: the athletes are curious to know right away where the race course is and

what condition the snow is in. Generally the entrants allow themselves two or three days of preparation before a race. When the teams have their lodging (which may range from rooms with five to 10 beds, to big hotels with single rooms) they begin to organize their skis and material. The bindings are remounted, torches for waxing begin to hum, a sound that mixes in with the usual question "When do we eat?"

Non-skiers may ask why the baggage is so cumbersome, but consider all the changes of clothing necessary not only for training and racing but also for the changes in climate. A team also needs to carry spare skis, poles, wax and other materials.

THE DAY BEFORE THE RACE

If the race is scheduled for Sunday, the team arrives at the place, for example, the Wednesday before. The athletes should train well on Thursday and Friday, during which time they should study the layout of the course and the condition of the snow. For a cross-country skier, knowing the race course is just as important as it is for a downhill skier. Even a race 50 km. (31 miles) long can be decided by just tenths of a second. An athlete who doesn't know the track can easily lose seconds and the delay builds up quickly to half a minute or more.

On Saturday, the day before the race, it is well to work out more slowly. The body needs a chance to recuperate. A skier training too intensely on the day before the race consumes too many carbohydrates from his system with negative consequences during the race. A person can build up a reserve of up to 4 hectograms (14 ounces) of glucose in the muscles and the liver. When you are resting and your meals are rich in carbohydrates (containing sugar), your body will create a reserve which assumes great importance during a race, because it will help maintain the blood sugar at a normal level. To function well, your body needs one gram (0.035 oz.) of sugar for each litre (1.05 quart) of blood. The Italian team follows the practice of drinking one or two glasses of lukewarm, sweetened orangeade before the race, a drink that is also given to the team members during the run over longer courses.

When the body works for a long period, the percentage of sugar in the blood begins to drop and the system calls on the reserve deposited in the muscles and the liver. If the system doesn't have a reserve at the beginning of a race, as can happen if you have trained too hard the day before and you haven't taken in sufficient quantities of carbohydrates, fatigue will inevitably overcome you.

Even an athlete who is aware of becoming tired can find himself suddenly in a crisis—it comes up like a slap in the face. The body is drained of energy, the legs hardly move, each step causes enormous fatigue, and you have continuous distress. If at that moment you can supply yourself with sugar, your body will recover rapidly; but it is important to avoid or at least anticipate the arrival of the crisis, in order not to be caught unprepared.

On the day before the competition, the team should ski the length of the track to become better acquainted with the terrain of the prepared course and the condition of the snow, and also because a well trained body needs to keep itself in motion. Many skiers, especially the younger ones, cover the course at full speed, with great ease, but the day after they pay for the effort by giving a mediocre performance in the race, and that at the cost of enormous fatigue. When the trainer advises them to expend less energy, they, of course, answer that they are not tired and that they feel great. Compare this with a car that has to cover 500 km. (300 miles) but has a gasoline supply for only 250 km. (150 miles). For the first 100 miles, the car can go at its maximum speed, but to arrive at its destination it still has to have gasoline for another 200 miles. An athlete, too, must have fuel for the desired distance, but he doesn't have a mechanical gauge to measure the content of his tank—he has to know how to recognize the condition of his own body.

During the evening before the race a certain widespread nervousness is normal—if the atmosphere was calm, that would be something to worry about! It is important that the athletes be nervous thinking about the next day's contest. This nervousness is part of the indispensable concentration. Every athlete has difficulty falling asleep and none even want to go to bed—it is nothing to worry about. If the skier has observed a well regulated routine in the preceding days and has slept well on previous nights, a little trouble sleeping the night before the competition doesn't preclude the possibility of turning in a brilliant performance.

Always on the evening before the race the athletes clean their skis and prepare them for waxing. They check their equipment and their racing numbers for their chests and backs which have already been distributed. They also study the order of departure. A skier wants to know where to find his opponents during a race: in this way he can evaluate his own time in respect to that of the other races. If he doesn't know his strongest opponents by sight, but only by name, it is important to learn and remember their departure numbers. Many young skiers have spoiled their chances by going after another opponent whom they believed to be a champion, only to discover at the finish line that they had done battle with a mediocre opponent.

The skiers also should acquaint themselves with the locations where they can find wax and spare material before departure, where the supply posts are situated along the course during the race, where the timers are, the places where skis and poles can be exchanged, and the people responsible for each of these places. For 10 and 15 km. (6 and 9 mile) races, supply posts are not ordinarily established. These are set up only for 30 and 50 km. (18.6 and 31 mile) or longer distance races. For the Olympics and worldwide races, these preparations are offered by a special organization. They use radio transmitters to give each athlete precise information about his time; for the 30 and 50 km. (18.6 and 31 mile) races supply posts are located at intervals of 5 km. (3 miles) or less. That doesn't mean that the skier must be supplied at each post: they are there if needed.

In regard to drinks taken during the run, an important rule to remember is: better to drink early than too late. To benefit from a drink taken in the last stretch of a long race, you should remember that the system needs at least 10 minutes to assimilate the sugar. A sugary drink won't benefit a skier when he is already in the shower so the last supply post should be at least a few kilometres (two miles or more) from the finish line. In the last stretch it offers at least moral support.

Every athlete must have found out his departure time to know when on the morning of the race it is opportune to eat breakfast. Eat calmly and be finished 2 or, even better, 3 hours before your departure.

THE DAY OF THE RACE

It is now the day of the race. Breakfast must not be too abundant. Your hearty meals should have been eaten the day and the evening before the race. For breakfast, the competitors should drink coffee with milk, or tea. They can eat bread, butter, jam, and in any event eggs, a little cheese or ham. Everyone asks questions about the temperature, about wax, about the weather. The hours preceding departure are hours of preparation and of nervousness.

PREPARATION OF THE SKIS

Waxing is an important chapter in the life of a cross-country skier; to become a champion in this department it is necessary to have long experience, to have made innumerable and systematic tests. Waxing is an individual operation and each athlete should do it on his own behalf, without confusing his ideas by listening too much to others.

At one time, coaches and assistants prepared the skis of the athletes with different types of wax which they secretly compounded themselves. Today, manufactured wax satisfies the needs of skiers for every type of snow. Each athlete must, therefore, find the wax most suitable for him, and the waxing done can vary greatly—depending on his weight, on technique and on style. A pair of skis that slides backwards for one person may give someone else sufficient adherence, yet allow him to gain speed when going downhill.

In every way, the best system for waxing well is to do a test with an extra pair of skis. Many skiers, however, are lazy and neglect to bring spare skis to try out on the course before the race.

Up to a point, it is possible for skiers to work together on waxing and exchange information. An athlete doesn't always have the time to acquaint

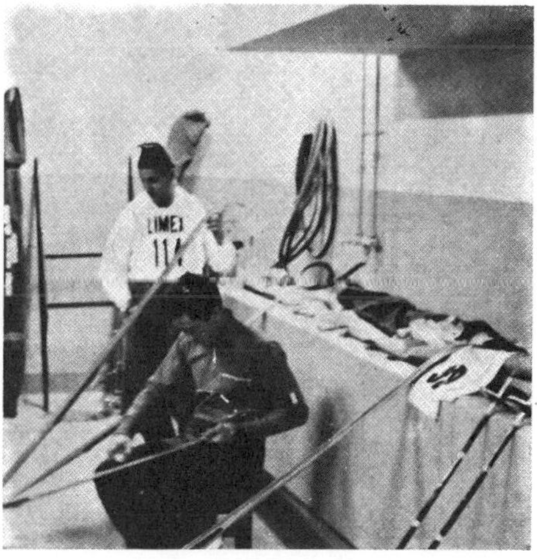

himself completely with the course so as to assemble precise data on the snow and the temperature. It is good in this case to send the coach, an assistant or a team member who isn't taking part in the race out on the course. Having found out all the data, they can be depended upon to transmit it as fast as possible to the participant by radio transmitter or in person, also giving information and opinions about the wax to be used. Each skier must then decide for himself.

Once your decision in regard to wax is made, don't listen any further to what others have to say. Be sure of your own ideas about the type of wax to use and, if you don't have this confidence, it is important that you have sufficient time to test your skis and to rewax them if necessary.

Many novices listen to too much advice from all sides and at the moment of departure leave with ten or more layers of wax on their skis. Your outcome in the race is likely to be poorer in this case than with a pair of skis not waxed at all.

ATTIRE

Now the moment to dress for the race has arrived. It is important to control your temperature and not to risk covering yourself with too little: if you have any doubts about how to dress, remember that in racing it is better to be too warm than too cold. When the temperature is moderate enough, you can ski in only racing pants without long underwear. If it is cold, "long johns" are an important item to keep your leg muscles warm and to impede the stiffening of the muscles all over the body. Many skiers prefer competing without gloves; but you must not risk freezing your fingers. If it is very cold, you also need to cover your ear lobes.

The three things to check carefully before departure are:

(1) that racing pants and underwear are not tied so tightly over your stomach that they might interfere with deep breathing during exertion;

(2) that the racing number is not bound too tightly around your upper body (again so as not to interfere with breathing) and that the bands over your shoulders are not too loose which might allow them to slide around interfering with your arm motions;

(3) that the bootlaces are tight, but not too tight, and are fastened securely enough that they won't untie during the run.

THE WARM-UP

The skier should start out for the racing field a considerable while before his departure time, especially if he is afraid that the wax may not be right and that he might have to change it. Every skier knows that he can't arrive at the departure point less than 20–25 minutes before his own "Go!"

Of this time, he uses 15–20 minutes for warming up; in the last 5 minutes he takes off his warm-up suit, saving several seconds for concentration before hearing the fateful words, "Ten seconds—five seconds—ready—set—go!"

The warm-up is essential for the cross-country skier. Many think that when you race over many kilometres or miles, that warm-up isn't so important believing that the first leg of the race will serve the same

Competitors nearing Mora, the finish line of Sweden's Wasalopp.

purpose. That just isn't accurate: before departing, a competitor must warm up well. Keep in mind that over a distance of 50 km., even a few tenths of a second can decide the race; a body not warmed up can easily lose those fractions right in the first few kilometres—with greater fatigue and waste of energy.

Another danger exists. The athlete who has not warmed up can easily have a muscular attack a short distance after leaving, a crisis that perhaps lasts only 5 or 10 minutes, until the body is warmed up and is accustomed to the intense activity. Nevertheless, these few minutes of crisis can cost dearly, maybe even a loss of 20–30 seconds compared to the time you would have made with the body well warmed up.

The warm-up for cross-country is slightly different than for other sports. You dress—over the racing uniform—in warm clothes that cover your legs, your whole chest and arms, and with gloves on your hands and a cap on your head. Your muscles must not be exposed to the cold at all or they will become stiff. Wearing these special clothes and performing energetically, it is easy to work up quite a sweat in 20–25 minutes; you, therefore, must be careful not to get too wet before leaving, because once having taken off the warm-up clothes you run the risk of freezing up in the first minutes of the race when your body hasn't yet reached its working temperature.

The warm-up, then, is performed in moderation: you should feel your heart beating stronger, ready to "shift gears" for the more tiring work to come—the race. Exaggerated muscular gymnastics are useless. It is sufficient to move enough to have loose, warm muscles ready for exertion.

During the warm-up period, you should also have your skis marked by the race officials. Moreover, you should check what is the exact course to be at departure and at the finish after the spectators are lined up along the track. There can, in fact, be variations in respect to the course followed in training.

CONCENTRATION BEFORE THE "GO!" SIGNAL

The last 15–20 minutes are full of concentration. No useless chatter, no joking with friends or spectators. You must pay attention to the departures to see what number is at the starting line so as not to lose your turn. You should be in visual contact with your team's assistant who is generally found near the starting point to help the members of the squad.

LONG
VYSOKÉ
MS 70
TATRY
69

THE CONDUCT OF THE RACE

Here then is the competitor at the moment of the "Go!" signal. Many people ask a skier, "What do you think about while you are racing along the course?" And a coach frequently hears the question, "What orders did you give the skier before he left?"

What the competitor thinks about is certainly an individual thing; often he just thinks about personal things, completely private, in relation to everyday life. A thought comes suddenly to mind, then leaves it, and meanwhile the effort continues in the rhythm of the race. Some situations always repeat themselves for all the competitors. After a few minutes of racing, you get the answer to the question, "How is the wax?"

122

A skier feels the skis "hold" at the moment that, in each stride, he starts pushing, and he feels the skis run quickly and easily within the track at the moment of gliding. The wax is good: he can hope that the race will continue well.

When a skier notices his skis slip backwards, or that they are not gliding fast—that means the wax is wrong. A competitor shouldn't let this upset him or jump to the conclusion that the race is lost; he has ahead of him, certainly, a tiring race, but he can tell himself that the other competitors have wax as bad as his. No one knows the final results until he arrives at the finish line.

When a problem with wax exists, it usually doesn't come up for only one competitor: the temperature can change during the race and the snow on the course may change its physical structure two or even three times (frozen first, then powdery, then wet). A skier shouldn't be spoiled to the point where he wants to run only on perfect snow; a real champion is able to win on whatever type of snow there is. It is important, therefore,

to possess great will power, besides physical strength and technical ability, and to always remember the maxim, "Don't give up." Anyone ready for major competition has to accept the fact that the chance of having good, rather than bad, snow conditions is about equal.

At the same time you consider the condition of the wax, you can start to evaluate your speed and time in respect to the other competitors. When the departures are made in pairs at intervals of one minute, you have an immediate means of comparison. When departures are made singly, every 30 seconds, a little time usually must elapse before you can see if you are gaining or losing ground in respect to the opponent who started half a minute before you. You should never look backwards—it disturbs the rhythm and the stability of your gait. If you turn back repeatedly, you run the risk of losing your balance and, thus, precious seconds.

Planning

The tactics that an athlete should adopt in modern racing, in which the times and separations are closer together, is this: *"Give everything that your body can give—Put forth your best effort right from the starting line."* It isn't possible to give a general scheme or grand plan for the conduct of a race, such as to depart with moderate rhythm, or to alternate bursts of effort with periods of rest. Whoever allows himself to be outshone by 20–30 seconds in the initial part of a race, however, makes it practically impossible to recover. It would perhaps be possible only in a race of more than 30 km. (18 miles).

Nevertheless, a skier can prearrange some tactics before the race, but remembering that the general rhythm of a race is high and that when he arrives at the place where he would have put on a burst of speed according to his plan, it might not be possible for him to augment his speed at all. On the contrary, it could happen that he will arrive at that point exactly at that moment when he finds himself in a muscular crisis so that his special effort will do no more than allow him to maintain the normal rhythm.

An athlete needs to be aware that the race also may not go along according to his plans: in that case, he must be able to improvise so as to overcome any problems with a minimum loss of time. During training he becomes familiar with the course, and so can think of an alternate spot where he can use a burst of speed.

In conclusion, it is advantageous to establish in your mind on how to run the race in a general way, but you must always be ready for the fact that the race can unfold differently than you expect. Your basic plan must be to give your best even at the beginning of the race. If you don't, there will always be another competitor ready to do it. To win, half-way measures won't do. Sometimes, after a skier has run the first stretch, he senses that it is a good day and that he has the race in the palm of his hand. With ease he catches up to other competitors and, when the moment is right, passes, leaving the others behind without feeling the least fatigue.

Days like this come and they seem almost unreal, almost as if you are intoxicated with strength and power even when the scoreboard at the finish line is in sight. Other days, instead, the effort is heavier and then it is important not to become discouraged. The race is more tiring, but you shouldn't think of dropping out. It may seem that way at the beginning and yet the finale will be easy. It is also possible that the race will be tiring from beginning to end, but the great champions win on these days also. You must, therefore, train your will power as well as your body.

You must give your best from the very start of the race, putting on extra bursts of effort to take advantage of the terrain or to pass another skier.

AID ON THE COURSE

The duty of the trainer or an assistant during a race usually doesn't directly influence the results. They are, however, entrusted with some particulars that can aid you to win a victory. They are the ones who see that reserve material is available at departure, who keep wax and torch ready for competitors who have to change wax before departure. These assistants should keep themselves at the disposal of the competitors without disturbing their concentration, their warm-up, or their general preparation for the race.

Along the course, it is their duty to establish points for time checks, supplies and spare material. From the point of view of the trainer, following the contest between the competitors along the course is an exciting thing: often he stands for hours, nervous and anxious in the cold, with a chronometer in hand, thermos bottles and a radio. He can not do much but wait, hoping for every member of his team engaged in the contest. A skier is nervous on his own account, while the trainer waits steadfastly next to the course and is tense for all of his team members in the race. The competitor rids himself of nervous tension by activity; the trainer must stand firm, without much chance to move about.

The trainer and his assistants are responsible for establishing points along the course for time checks, supplies, and spare equipment.

A chronometer and the sheet listing the departure order of the competitors enable the assistants along the course to give their skier an idea of his comparative time and position.

It is important, however, that he does a good job of the aid he is permitted to extend to the skiers in the race. Knowing the order of departure and with the help of the chronometer, or with reports from the radio, he is able to give an individual competitor an idea of his position and his time in comparison to the others, tell him who is in the lead, the distance between him and the leader, the distance between him and the competitor immediately ahead. Some skiers also ask, before leaving, to have information about a particular opponent; but you can understand how it is not always possible to give all these details on the progress of a competitor. The trainer should, therefore, decide which are, at the moment, the important reports and give them in a loud, clear voice. The athlete may be tired or cold and wearing earmuffs. The shouts of the spectators can cover the words. It is better to shout too loud than risk having your team member miss the report. Moreover, a trainer must be certain that the information is exact: no information is better than an incorrect report.

To make the job of timing the progress of a race easier and more secure, the trainer can prepare various time plans that will help him to read with ease the time differences between the competitors. On each plan assign the time "0" to a specific athlete, then graduate the times of the others in comparison to him. It is important for the assistants along the course to place themselves in spots that are tactically advantageous. The competitors should know before leaving where the control spots for their own team are located.

The assistants should always be alert to single out reports that can be of interest to their own team. It is important, for example, to notice

82
LuxorTV

For the trainer, a race means careful preparation and patient waiting. For the athlete, it is a hard battle, not without an occasional fall.

when an athlete on your team is tired and fails to go after a less able opponent of a very inferior class. Even if fatigued he must be encouraged to pass this adversary. It can happen also that an athlete falls in behind a well known champion who he expects will place high in the race; the assistant in this case should note what the true position of the champion is, and if it corresponds to a place among the front runners. Maybe on this day the champion is not in the mood, yet the others follow behind him, pleased with themselves at the ease of keeping pace with such a man. In this case, it is important to explain the situation to the skier and encourage him to pass the champion and to increase his speed.

Assistants should also be ready with spare material, that is skis and poles.

In big races, in addition to the timing posts set up in tactically pre-chosen spots, the officials also set up posts given over to reserve equipment, generally where there are difficult or fast slopes.

Breaking a ski or pole is a disagreeable occurrence, but when the competitor knows it is possible to exchange material, he doesn't abandon the contest.

During the 1964 Olympics, the Swedish skier, Assar Rönnlund, won the silver medal in the 50-km. after having broken a ski and exchanging it first with a spectator, then at the Swedish reserve-material post. According to international rules, race officials mark the skis of each competitor before departure and he is allowed to change only one of them in the

Assar Rönnlund leading the Swedish relay team to victory in the 1964 Olympics at Innsbruck, Austria.

course of the race. The ski that is broken and exchanged can be replaced a second time, but you must arrive at the finish line wearing at least one of the skis with which you left.

For an important race, the organizers establish refreshment stops in addition to the timing and spare materials posts. It is advantageous also to prearrange team supply posts. At these "team posts," the skiers know exactly what they are drinking: a good many skiers, in a moment of fatigue, take a drink from the official post that they are unaccustomed to. The result is an upset stomach, and the day is lost. The official posts are also frequently crowded. Several competitors arrive at the same time and have to wait for a drink. Instead, at the control post of your own team, you can get a drink "on the run," generally from friends who are also skiers and know how to move with ease and speed along the course in a way that makes you lose the least possible time.

The composition of the beverages that the skiers drink may vary from one team to another. The base is always sugar dissolved in a liquid (orangeade, coffee, tea, etc.). Sometimes there are skiers who want other things as, for example, sugared orange slices, but this happens rather seldom. The assistants who organize the supply posts for long distance races should remember that it is better to prearrange too many posts than too few. Athletes should remember that it is better to drink too early than too late.

The work of the assistant on the course ends when the last member of his team has passed. He then closes his pack, puts his watch in his pocket, gets on the track and sets out for the finish line. Maybe he will have to cover several kilometres on skis, and meanwhile he thinks about how the race has gone for the boys and what the results will be after so much work and tension. Many times, this is the very moment that one questions the reason for this merry-go-round of racing with all its related tension. Perhaps the reason is that everyone has inside him a competitive instinct, more or less developed. On the racing field you find an outlet for this tension: for those who don't participate actively in competitive sports, it is stimulating just to be where the action takes place.

AFTER THE FINISH LINE

High level sport and the champions who practice it do have some detractors: and, in truth, many of their negative arguments are plausible. But aren't there maybe things to improve all aspects of daily life? Any negative side of this sport is submerged in all the positive aspects that it

The classic pose of the victor.

offers. Races, training, travelling all over the world, meeting different people, friendship across borders and with people of different political persuasions, life in the open air—these are all things that have value and a wide-awake athlete can transform every day into a new lesson. If he uses his sports experience wisely, it can have great value for his future. Past races are something for a retired champion, finished with racing, to remember well. It isn't proper to sit and twiddle your thumbs and think that money and future security will arrive by chance. When you are finished racing, it is time to do battle off the course as you have done on the track and every skier should take advantage of what he has learned and the reputation he has earned in the years of active sport.

Turning back to the end of the race, the assistant coming along the track can allow his mind to wander freely. When the race is finished, the trainer sets out for the finish line that the public, the competitors and the race officials are abandoning. On the score board are the results of the race. The trainer looks around for his boys, but he prefers not to find anyone. An athlete who has worked up a sweat should take a shower right away, dry himself and dress in warm, dry clothes. Many contests remain to take part in, so it is unwise to risk getting a cold. How many young athletes, right after the race, take a shower and then immediately go outside among the people, with a wet head, wearing party clothes and no cap because they think it spoils their appearance. This is something a trainer should watch for carefully. Skiers absolutely should not go out in the cold with a wet head (from water or from sweat). It is not worth risking an illness when you have ahead of you so many beautiful contests on the race track.

At the very end is the awarding of prizes, and sometimes a "friendship party" among the skiers. For the trainer, the presentation of awards is generally a tiring business. He has seen too much of it. All the same, it is clear that for the young, winning athletes, these can be great moments. The real reward for the trainer comes earlier when, with chronometer in hand at the edge of the course, he realizes that the skier on whom he has pinned his hopes is handling the course according to expectations, or even better.

The contest is over. Now it is already a memory to be put with others more distant. New trips, new contests, quickly—too quickly—the competitive season comes to an end. The competitors put away their racing boots and winter clothes, they clean their skis of old wax and put them in bags.

You start then to think about the next training and racing season: Olympics, World Championships of the future; and in mind too are the past competitions. Through the memories of cross-country skiers file the names of the great races. The athlete who has once lived this experience can never forget the thousands of spectators and friends who with joyous excitement have spurred him on to battle, maybe even to victory.

First place, a moment of joy that he will long remember.

Pre-Season Training

Many people imagine that training for cross-country starts when the first snow falls. This is understandable, because few are aware of how hard an athlete must train today, and this is particularly true for the cross-country skier.

The modern athlete by now recognizes the fact that his is year-round training. This doesn't mean that a cross-country skier has to go around a cross-country course twelve months a year, even if this were a possibility. The skier's year is divided in two parts—six months of summer and six of winter.

The winter months, in northern temperate zones from the beginning of November to the end of April, are taken up in training on snow and actual competitions. In the six months that are normally without snow, you put skis aside and go for other types of activity. What you can never put aside is training. The basis for the winter's results is laid during the summer. It is impossible with the high level of modern competition to succeed at an international level only with training on snow.

The major part of the preparation suggested in this chapter is for the athlete who participates in competitions. Even for a beginner who loves cross-country, though, this year-round training will be valuable. You don't need to devote the same intensity and time to it as a beginner as is demanded from the serious competitor.

The final cross-country race usually takes place in the middle of April, many times with a spring sun more appropriate to swimming than to winter sports, and it is understandable why, at this point, an athlete is tired of skiing and contests. Five or six months of travelling in addition to anywhere from 30 to 50 or more races over distances varying from

10–85 km. (6–53 miles) tire a person notably. The skiers have the right to hang up their skis and rest.

This doesn't mean, however, that training can be interrupted—it is certainly not a period in which the main activity is lying around in bed, sleeping and eating until the first snowflakes fall again.

Some skiers maintain that in this period they work hard at their jobs and so don't have the need for training, but they are wrong. Even for those who do heavy manual work it is important to continue training the body with races, gymnastics and other sports. It may seem more logical for a skier with a sit-down job to have to continue training than one who does manual work. But a risk connected with manual work is that the athlete, lacking all-round training, may become too stiff, his muscles may contract, and he may not exert his heart and lungs sufficiently.

Training means increasing the functional capacity of the heart,

Condition training, to maintain your skill and staying power, is essential during the part of the year when you cannot train on snow.

circulatory system, lungs, muscles and ligaments. For the cross-country skier, the most important thing is the capacity to inhale large amounts of air during exertion so as to absorb greater quantities of oxygen.

CONDITION TRAINING

Training done without skis is called "condition training."

Great athletes in every sport may be—or have been—great phenomena of conditioning. But none of them would be able to become a cross-country champion without special training for this sport.

Conditioning consists of activity that the skier takes up when he finishes skiing at the end of April, some game or sport that he can engage in several times a week in his own surroundings, even in his own home. It needn't be a strenuous effort, something more in the category of entertainment. You can play tennis or handball or soccer or swim and run; in any case, as an athlete in long-distance sport, you should now and again take long walks or runs for condition training.

During the spring, an athlete rests his body and mind after the tiring competitions of winter so that when he starts to work hard again, his body is better prepared than if he had remained at complete rest. Continuing this way, year after year, it is easier to increase the severity of training to raise your skill and staying power to an ever higher level. A skier who has to start over again every year can get to a certain level of performance but not much beyond.

Athletes from about 16 to 24 years old can come back to top form easily enough, even after a period of complete inactivity, but every year the difficulty increases. For older athletes there is the risk of not succeeding before the start of competition. Even so, young skiers should not rest completely. For them it is important to learn right away to accustom the body to year-round training.

Toward summer you intensify your training. Participate in sports more times a week, but lightly and pleasantly, in short, with ease.

At the start of summer it is time to think about true training. Here it is possible to decide case by case: it depends on the age and type of athlete.

With training done over a long period you develop a more stable form for winter. An athlete 16 to 18 years old can, certainly, get in shape in just one month, but with short and intense training, the resulting form is less stable. In any event, his training doesn't have to be as long and intense as for older skiers.

For some athletes over 30 it isn't enough to begin training in mid-summer: they should start even before summer begins. Others between 20 and 22, on the contrary, are not so far out of shape and can start in late summer or even early autumn. Early summer, however, is good for the majority of skiers.

During the summer months, skiers in training can make light runs in the country, or run on a track for 100–200–400–800 and 1,500 metres (about 100 yards to slightly less than a mile). Greater distances, from 1,500 metres onward, are seldom done on the track but on open ground or along roads.

To run on a track for distances greater than 1,500 metres calls for special training; skiers on snow-covered courses use their leg muscles differently. This doesn't mean that a skier can't learn to run well for long distances on a track. Many of the better Norwegian and Swedish cross-country skiers also take part in their respective national track meets. Most are careful, however, not to compete too much during the summer to avoid building up physical and psychological tension.

Besides running, cross-country skiers train in the other track and field events, such as the long-jump, the high jump, shot put and the obstacle course. They also play tennis, swim, do gymnastics, play various kinds of ball games—almost all the summer sports are suitable.

It is good, however, to understand the reason for performing in a certain sport, that is, to know what you want to achieve. For example, for those who want to become cross-country skiers, boxing or wrestling is of little value; rather, running 100 metres (a little more than 100 yards) on a track develops speed and leg muscles, and even the heart and lungs get a good workout—all useful elements for winter. Races twice or four times as long are run in part for speed, but here the workout for the heart and lungs is more important and increases even more, naturally, for the greatest distances. Training for these distances is generally done in intervals. This means that you run the distance several times, alternating each run with a period of rest which varies in duration in proportion to the degree of training (from a few seconds to 3 to 4 minutes). The speed over the distance also depends directly on the degree of training. It can be full speed but, generally, the athlete runs at 70–80 per cent of his capacity.

Long or broad jump, shot put and obstacle races are done as exercises and in these the athlete should work easily, but with strength and speed. All these exercises contribute to the development of strength, agility and speed that will serve later, in other ways, in skiing.

Running is the basis for cross-country summer training. Shot put, high jump, hurdles and broad jump are all activities that develop strength and agility.

Regular gymnastic exercises are done to develop individual quickness and harmony; a part serves to develop muscular strength, but this only to the degree that results in strength useful for cross-country skiing.

Weight-lifting within certain limits can be useful to the skier but he must know the correct procedure. There is the danger of developing a muscular system which serves only partially for cross-country. With a muscle system that is too bulky, the skier increases his weight, and finds himself with useless pounds to carry around. Hard but well done gymnastics which include chinning, climbing a rope with the arms and other exercises just for the arms are certainly preferable to weight-lifting.

Many skiers also do elastic or steel spring exercises especially to give the arms extra work. Generally, the training of a skier is concerned principally with the leg muscles, but you must also think about the arms

As the summer progresses, training must become more intense, with organized gymnastic exercises.

Training with weights can be a good alternative when it is difficult to take part in other muscle-developing activities.

Ordinary summer sports and games are useful for keeping a competitive skier in shape as well as fun for the participants.

because the work with the poles is an important element in cross-country skiing.

Swimming releases physical and psychological tension after hard training. Ball games (tennis, basketball, handball, soccer, baseball) are strength-building exercises in part, but they also serve as training in speed and agility and they are also entertaining, which is of value since to continue running down the road mile after mile can become boring.

During the summer months you can also participate in a session of training on skis if possible. To find snow in the summer, it is necessary to go up to an altitude where the air is rarefied and the oxygen is scarce. But this training isn't really for cross-country: it is downhill training using downhill skis. It is fun for cross-country skiers and has value because modern cross-country race courses present many challenging descending slopes that can become even more difficult with frozen snow. In winter, it is often difficult for cross-country skiers to find time and terrain to practice downhill skiing, so they are beginning to do it in summer or autumn.

TESTS AND HEALTH

During strenuous training, athletes everywhere try to verify what condition they have attained and for this they undergo a physiological test. For this test you need to have available a special apparatus, the ergometercycle.

The ergometercycle is, substantially, a bicycle without wheels, on which you activate the pedals with a certain rhythm. The pedals can be braked by means of a device with seven different settings, which correspond to as many different tables. Measuring the heartbeat after a pre-established exertion, trainers can calculate the level of development for an individual athlete.

As an example, you approach the test with the brake in the third position. Start with 6 minutes to warm up and then do 6 minutes with the brake in fourth position. The pulse beat is measured each minute. The value that is of interest is that obtained after the 6 minutes with the control in fourth position. Six minutes is the time required for the heartbeat to stabilize. Beyond 6 minutes, the pulse doesn't vary even at the 8- or 10-minute check.

After his test, an athlete knows the count of his own stabilized heartbeat. This value is strictly individual, and it cannot be said that someone who has a count of 120 beats a minute is a better skier than someone who measures 140 beats. Each athlete should direct his training in such a way that the count goes down. The athlete with 120 beats should train for 115 beats or less. Someone with a pulse of 140 should strive for 135 or even lower.

The test is made once a month and, if the curve of values descends, you need only continue training calmly. If, instead, the values stay the same it is better to try to find out what is wrong: the cause may be poor training rather than a health problem.

While this special equipment is not so readily available, anyone can check his own approximate level of training by measuring his heartbeat in the morning as soon as he awakens in bed for several consecutive days in order to establish an average. Do this every month to obtain a measurement curve.

The ergometercycle and a weight scale are means for checking and evaluating the effect of your training.

With about 60 beats a minute in July, 50 in October and 45 in December you can be sure that your training has brought results. Remember, though, that this is only a small positive sign and the values are highly individual.

Naturally, smoking and drinking are prohibited for a champion. Of the two, smoking is the most dangerous. If an athlete occasionally drinks a glass of wine or beer, it will do no great harm, but smoking is absolutely forbidden. Drugs of any kind should not need to be mentioned—they are too dangerous for anyone, athlete or not. Remember the importance of a visit to your doctor. For champions, constant medical supervision is necessary.

A person who finds the will to begin training hard to reach a sporting goal almost certainly enjoys good health. But modern training is tiring: it is pointless to take risks. Most important is that you take care of your heart, lungs and stomach—also your teeth. An athlete should visit his doctor at least once a year for a checkup and go to the dentist at least twice a year.

Many athletes neglect their teeth and this can be costly. When starting the competitive season, skiers put maximum stress on the body and it is easy under these circumstances for badly-cared-for teeth to start up infections that can involve the whole lymphatic system, and so the season is ruined.

In a team at the national level this medical supervision is obligatory, and it is of noteworthy psychological help for every athlete to know that he is in good health while in training.

Unfortunately, there are some who exaggerate this medical supervision. They go to the doctor for every minor upset and ask for medicine and pills in quantity. Remember that the most important thing is to know that all is well; when you are sure of this, it is pointless to rely on pills. When a person has a continuous need for medicine, he should ask himself if he is really in shape to continue training at a high level.

Naturally, there are cases in which an athlete may need medicine but doctors who work with athletes should be careful to administer it only in case of absolute necessity, and not heed imaginary maladies. The best medicine is that of living, eating and sleeping in a normal way, without allowing oneself foolish notions. A champion must be firm with himself and live with method: "I can eat—sleep—train—run, in any place—at any hour—in any weather: nothing can disturb my psychological stability."

STRENUOUS TRAINING

In early autumn, the team goes to places where there is a forest suitable for running and long walks. Where gyms are seldom available, training in gymnastics can continue outdoors on open ground with the equipment that you find in the place—a branch for chinning, big rocks to jump over, steep slopes to jump down–the athletes assisting themselves with ski poles.

An apparatus used by many skiers in gymnastic training is a bicycle inner tube. Some of them are joined together so that they are 2 metres or more (about 7 feet) in length and you pass the resulting band around a tree or a fixed hook. Gripping an end in each hand, you start gymnastic exercises that become ever more difficult and tiring since the resistance of the tubes becomes greater the farther back you move.

Another piece of equipment that has had widespread use in the last few years is the so-called "ski-roller." This piece of equipment develops the

To vary your warm-weather training, spend some days in the countryside. Bicycle inner tubes wrapped around a tree or a post make a fine apparatus for developing your arm muscles.

Various types of "ski-rollers" have been developed to simulate the movements of skiing on dry land. The metal variety above is from East Germany, the wooden version below from Norway.

same arm and shoulder muscles in the same way they are used on the course. Using it is also good for the heart and lungs. Besides, it is diverting for the athletes. Forcing yourself to "ski" along at a constant speed without strain serves best to improve your technique.

The ski-roller is especially useful for an athlete who may have been injured and not yet recovered sufficiently to run. It is also helpful for younger skiers who are not yet able to follow a full schedule of strenuous training.

A period of group training for a team should consist of at least 8 consecutive days, but not more than 14 days. The rest between one period of training and another during the summer months can be from 6 to 10 days, and later, in autumn, of 4 or at the most 6 days.

The author and fellow trainer Lennart Larsson trying out some ski-rollers.

All these suggestions are directed to the optimum in training conditions. Anyone who really wants to can find the opportunity to train at home, on the streets and paths that are familiar to him. Problems of training terrain affect champions more than others. Their training has to be done in a severe way, under tension. They know that when winter arrives they have to get results. On streets that are too hard they can break legs and, in fact, often sustain injuries, accidents and inflammations of various types.

NINE TYPICAL DAYS

Here are some examples of plans for a standard day of training during different months and periods. They constitute only a basic outline and are not meant to be followed to the letter, rather they are to be adapted to the people and terrain at your disposal.

Example #1

A plan for a month in midsummer, in the course of a training session on snow with downhill skis, in a locality situated 3,000 metres (nearly 10,000 feet) above sea level; in the valley below—at an elevation of about 1,400 metres (about 4,500 feet)—there are roads and paths for running on foot.

8:00–9:00—free downhill practice on downhill skis;
9:00–10:00—lessons from a teacher (progression of training on downhill skis);
10:00–11:00—free practice;
12:00–2:00—lunch break;
2:00–3:30—rest;
3:30–5:00—light cross-country run in the valley on roads or paths and light gymnastics (substitute tennis occasionally).

This schedule can be varied. Even at 3,000 metres it is possible to do technical training with cross-country skis. Cross-country training should be conducted moderately—not excessively at this altitude. The run in the afternoon, scheduled for an hour and a half, doesn't mean that you must run continuously: it is good, instead, to alternate running, walking and gymnastics. At times an athlete may feel himself in shape to run for an hour and a half without interruption.

Example #2

A schedule for midsummer, at a sports area with a track for running, a gym, swimming pool and with terrain suitable for cross-country races (on foot, not skis).

You should note that for a cross-country skier it is always better to find open terrain; it is also good to have a sports field, small meadows, a road. You must keep track of the distance covered rather than the time used up. When you have at your disposal both a sports field and open terrain it is advisable to alternate their use. For training on the track it is better to use a stop watch. Run partly on the grass inside the track, in part on the track itself. Wear track shoes when running on the track.

In the morning you should get up and eat quite a while before the start of training. If you are to report at the field at 10:00, it is good to eat breakfast at 8:00.

10:00–12:30—the schedule is divided this way:

(1) 20 minutes of easy running on the grass in sneakers;

(2) 15–20 minutes of gymnastics (the order is settled day by day) which consist fundamentally of:

(a) arm movements—head and upper torso—legs (here the idea is to work with ease and agility);

(b) strong arm movements—leg—abdomen—back (here the idea is to develop muscular strength);

(c) alternate the preceding exercises, or mix them with sprints, jumps of various kinds, going over the leather horse or other obstacles, vertical exercises on the hands, turning and somersaulting the body freely. You can make up a different routine for each athlete: the important thing is that in these 15–20 minutes of gymnastics each works effectively;

(3) run slowly for 1,500–2,000 metres (about a mile) on the track wearing track shoes;

(4) 20 minutes of intensive training in technical disciplines (shot put, broad jump, pole vault). The important thing is that the training is continuous, not interrupted after each section to sunbathe, chat with friends, etc.;

(5) 20 minutes of getting around small blockades or holes, fast sprints of short distances of 25–40 metres (about 100 feet). Clock the runs.

(6) 15–20 minutes of interval training over 400 metres (about 1,300 feet). Run the distance 3 to 6 times checking your time with the stop watch. The speed is decided each time (it can be faster or slower depending on the day and the ability of the athlete);

(7) 15 minutes of jogging on the grass;

From 12:30–3:00—lunch and rest;

3:00–5:00—swimming or basketball.

Anyone who doesn't know how to swim should learn. Those who know how can use swimming as part of their training, covering distances of 200 to 2,000 metres (about 650 feet to a little more than a mile). The lungs are well exercised in this way without tiring you too much to finish what you started in the morning.

On the other hand, it is also important to exercise on the track for longer distances; on days following that described in Example #2 you can follow Example #3 or, alternatively, Example #4.

Example #3

Another schedule for midsummer.

In the morning, take a fast hike of 20–25 km. (12–15 miles). After having covered half the distance, start a slow run. It is good to follow an itinerary that includes streets, small roads and paths in order to conduct the training on varied terrain.

In the afternoon: rest.

Example #4

Yet one more schedule for midsummer.

In the morning, do cross-country racing (on foot) on a course 3,000 metres (almost 10,000 feet) long. Run the course from three to five times at intervals. You should also do gymnastics as listed in Example #2.

In the afternoon: swimming or basketball.

Example #5

This schedule corresponds to Example #2, but is suitable for the end of summer. The location is again a sports area.

(1) run on grass: start with 10 minutes of slow running; then, without interrupting the continuity, 3–5 minutes of fast running; then again 10 minutes of slow running; and finally 3–5 minutes of fast running;

(2) 6–10 minutes of jogging, with a 50 metre dash (a little more than 50 yards) every minute;

(3) gymnastic exercises, as in Example #2, but intensified;

(4) 10 minutes of slow running over low obstacles;

(5) 1,500–2,000 metres (about 2,000 yards) of slow running on the track wearing track shoes;

(6) run 800 metres (872 yards) three times on the track wearing track

shoes, never in poorer time than 2 minutes 40 seconds (naturally a better time depends on the ability of each athlete). After each run of 800 metres, run 100 timed metres at maximum speed;

(7) 20–30 minutes of individual training in technical disciplines;

(8) 10–15 minutes of jogging on the grass.

The whole routine can be completed in $2\frac{1}{2}$ hours but, if necessary, you can prolong the time a little. At point (7) you should observe how tired the athlete is. If after running on the track his legs are too tired, it isn't advisable to start training in the long jump. In midsummer an athlete is still at the beginning of his preparation, and he should always be careful, but that care shouldn't be based on laziness.

The morning schedule is to be followed as in Example #2 by lunch, rest, and, in the afternoon, swimming or basketball.

When the season is farther along, in autumn, the woods are waiting for the skiers: there is still no snow but you can try out the terrain of winter's contests. It is another step forward.

Example #6

A schedule for early autumn over a terrain with woods and rolling meadows. If you are unable to find woods and meadows, run on dirt roads or, as a last resort, even on asphalt roads.

Morning schedule:

(1) cross-country race of 5 km. (3 miles)—to warm up;

(2) exercises (as in the other examples) for 10–25 minutes, at times very strenuous, other times less so;

(3) six uphill runs, 36–60 metres (about the same in yards) long;

(4) 2,000 metres ($1\frac{1}{4}$ miles) of cross-country racing, clocked and repeated three times—once at maximum speed, the others at regular time;

(5) another cross-country run on a 5-km. (3-mile) course, with varying speed.

Follow this with lunch and rest. In the afternoon, play some ball games. Baseball offers many short sprints and is fun besides.

Example #7

This is for a day in autumn, following that in Example #6.

In the morning, the routine can consist of a fairly hard run in the woods and mountains for a distance of 20–30 km. (12–18 miles).

In the afternoon, rest.

Example #8

Here is a schedule for a day in late autumn. It is similar to Example #6, but for harder training.

In the morning:

(1) cross-country run of 5 km. (3 miles)—to warm up;

(2) 15–20 minutes of hard gymnastics;

(3) cross-country race of 2,000 metres ($1\frac{1}{4}$ miles) with a fairly fast pace (for those who want to make the routine harder, they can run the 2,000 metres two or three times against a stopwatch);

(4) ten sprints on the grass for 100–200 metres (slightly more in yards);

(5) 3–6 runs of 20–600 metres up a fairly steep incline;

(6) cross-country race of 5–10 km. (3–6 miles).

Then have lunch and rest. In the afternoon do some activity such as baseball or volleyball.

Example #9

This is for a day in late autumn following that of Example #8.

In the morning, training can consist of running on paths in the woods and mountains for a distance of 25–35 km. (15–21 miles). The run can be clocked.

In the afternoon, rest.

KEEP YOUR SCHEDULE FLEXIBLE

The nine examples above show how the training schedule can be toughened up as the competitive season approaches. It is important to remember, though, not to follow a written routine blindly. When I went out with the Italian team I always had a paper in my pocket with a schedule (similar to one of those described) written out on it. But each time, to start off the training session, I had to evaluate whether the routine was

excessive or too modest for the day's condition. I asked myself: how is the weather? what terrain is available? how are the athletes? what should be changed in my schedule?

The body is capable of sustaining much harder training than you might think: you don't have to pull back the moment you notice the first signs of fatigue. Feeling tired after heavy training doesn't mean that you are ill, assuming, of course, that you are in good health to start with. Few moments are as fine as when an athlete, dead tired after the hardest training, can let himself fall into bed to rest.

This is then, in general, the scheme of preparation for team training. The schedules are set up day by day, but in a way that allows for the most possible variation. The switch from short dashes on the track to walking or running the 40 km. (24 miles) in the mountains, from running on flat ground to running on steep terrain are notable changes. There are many possibilities for making up schedules as you will discover.

Naturally, for an athlete who wants to train by himself, staying close to home and maybe even carrying on with a tiring job as well, it is difficult to carry out such a plan. I have simply set down the way that my experience has shown to produce the best results. Anyone who has the interest and the desire can organize a schedule based on these ideas, fitting it in with his normal daily life and taking into account the demands of his work.

After a day's work it can be good and even restful to do a little varied training even if you are tired, if it is dark outside or if the weather is bad. Young people who have ambition and desire always find in sports a goal to achieve.

The Equipment

Some of the equipment has changed dramatically in the last few years. Manufacturers have successfully developed fiberglass skis, including, most recently, skis that require no wax. The usual wood bottom is still the most common but the artificial bottom is coming more into use.

A comparison of manufacturer's specifications reveals that most competition skis weigh from 1,100 to 1,250 grams (2 lbs. 7 oz. to 2 lbs. 12 oz.). It's possible, of course, to find skis in the stores weighing even 1,300–1,400 grams and more (upwards of 3 lbs.). Also the length is important. It normally ranges from 205–215 cm., and 220 cm. for a particularly tall and heavy person. (This is about 82 to 88 inches. Cross-country skis are sold in the U.S., however, according to their metric lengths.)

It is impossible to say that a particular brand of ski is best. Each person has to try them for himself and to choose based on his own experience. It is interesting to note that a decade ago, the conviction prevailed that the skis had become too light. In spite of this, their weight has been reduced still further. Also the bindings and poles are a little lighter.

The boots and bindings most commonly used have remained basically the same, in the last few years. However, manufacturers are developing a modification that may receive more widespread use. The "rat trap" bindings (see pages 118-120), with holes in the front ends of the soles on the boots and pins on the skis, have been altered. The new design has extended tabs on the boots that fit into slots on the bindings. The boots themselves more resemble street running shoes (sneakers), and some of them have nylon uppers, replacing the usual leather.

Until a few years ago, poles made of wood or artificial material were not very widespread. The best were made of bamboo or small layers of wood glued together. Today, metal poles are the best and those of bamboo are

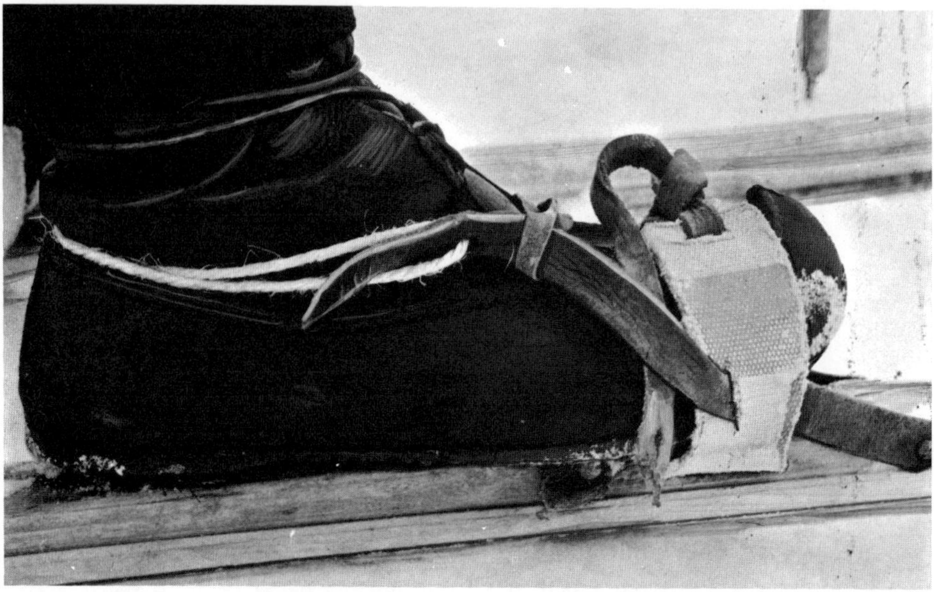

Not too many years ago, it was still possible to find old skiers still using shoes and bindings of this type.

considered out of style. Nevertheless, the choice of one type over another is completely up to the individual. Finding good equipment for cross-country skiing isn't difficult. All the sporting goods shops in the world stock whatever is new in this field. Cross-country skiers who are using old equipment would find it amazing to go into a sporting goods store and compare their gear with the new things for sale.

The pieces of equipment required for the serious cross-country skier or for anyone else who does touring with cross-country skis are as follows:

SKIS

Cross-country skis should be light. Even inexpensive models today weigh from 1,400–1,500 grams (about 3–3¼ lbs.) a pair without bindings. A pair of downhill skis, by comparison, weighs from 5–6 kilograms (about 11–13 lbs.). Cross-country skis should be flexible and strong, to respond to the wishes of the skier, adapting without breaking to the undulation of the terrain. Finally, they should be made of a material that allows the application of wax, that is, the base wax called "Grundvalla" (the various

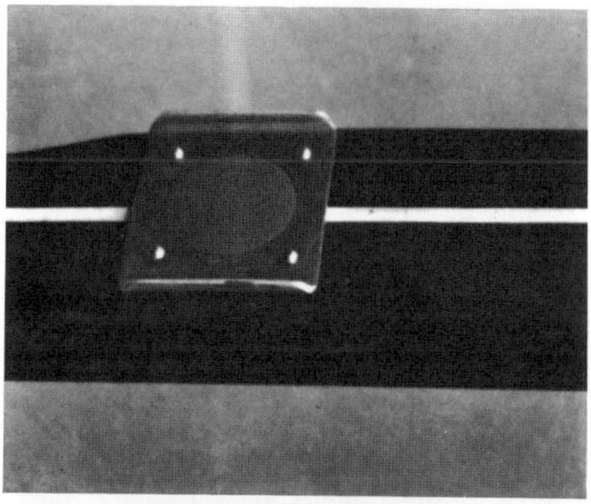

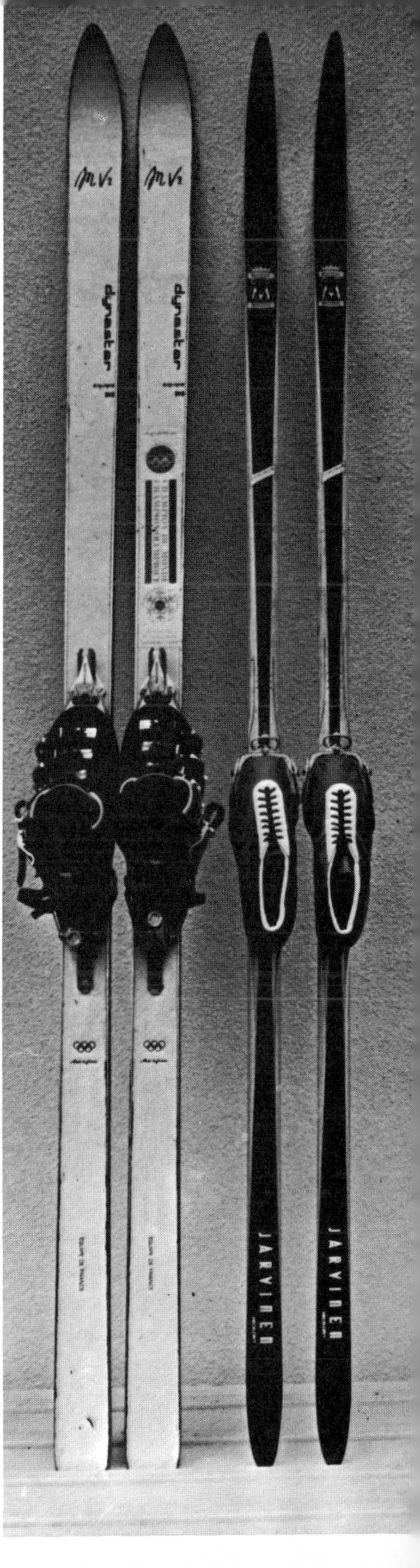

Modern boots, bindings and skis for cross-country and downhill skiing.

waxes are known throughout the world by their original Scandinavian names). This wax is made to penetrate into the wood with heat, and the other waxes are applied instead with a piece of cork or a warm iron.

In the last few years, competition skiers have been using skis made of fiberglass with a "P-Tex" base. These skis are considerably less fragile and also faster than the traditional skis. The waxless ski has also recently begun to be used in competition. In one type of waxless ski, two thin strips of mohair are attached to the base of the ski under the foot, a variation on the old practice of putting sealskin under the skis for ascending a slope. Another variety of waxless ski has a pattern cut at an angle that creates small ridges to prevent slipping backwards. Manufacturers are experimenting with embedding small chips of mica in the ski base.

The usual length for competition skis is 210 cm. regardless of the height and weight of the skier, but smaller skiers can use skis 205 cm. long, taller and heavier athletes skis from 215–220 cm. long. The shorter skis are lighter which is an advantage, but the longer skis stay on the track better and may be faster.

In the last few years the manufacturers have tried to make cross-country skis as narrow as possible, but they have by now reached the limit and the results are possibly too fragile. Some manufacturers build them laminated in the middle with very light dry wood; others create in the inside a series of small canals, both efforts to reduce the weight by even a few grams. But up to what point can these skis withstand the force of an athlete during a race? To save just a few grams, the builders were obliged to diminish the width. At the point where the tip flattens out, racing skis are now about 52 mm. (2 inches) wide. A downhill ski at the same point measures about 87 mm. (nearly 3½ inches). Moreover, the narrow ski on a "soft" track sinks in more easily, braking the glide ahead.

The camber (or "bridge") of a ski must be in relation to the weight of the skier. A lightweight skier shouldn't use skis with a high camber and vice versa, so as to obtain a better glide. The camber also affects the waxing—if it is too high you will very quickly use up the wax on the tip and on the tail and these parts will then exert a braking action even though the wax under your foot remains intact. If the camber is insufficient, the opposite occurs—the wax under your foot is used up and that on the tip and the tail remains nearly intact.

Old-time skiers view the modern skis with wonder when they remember theirs of 50 or 60 years ago that were four metres or more long (more than 13 feet).

EDSBYNS
EDSBYNS

These cross-country skis so reduced in weight and size are not intended for touring, but even here you need lighter skis than for downhill skiing. Long tours with heavy skis require outstanding strength, especially in the knees.

BINDINGS

The cross-country skier should have "bindings," as the fastenings for holding the toe of the boot firmly on the ski are called, that allow him to raise and lower his heels. This freedom of movement is some disadvantage on a descending course, but not as much as the disadvantage would be if you had to ski up a slope with your heels locked to the skis.

The most common bindings applied to cross-country skis are called "rottefella" or "rat trap" bindings. They consist of a metal mounting with three or four pins pointing up at the front. The front part of the soles of the boots have four holes corresponding to the pins on the bindings. You place your boots into the mounting so that the pins slide into the corresponding holes which hold them tightly. To catch them even more firmly, you lower a lever which fastens into a clamp fastened to the ski several centimetres (a few inches) in front of the boot.

There are some variations on this type of binding but the basic principle remains the same. The rat trap type is the most used binding today. It is also suitable for touring, where it is also possible to use a "Kandahar" or "cable" binding, with the strap going behind the heel. The metal strap can be arranged in a way that leaves the heel free in order

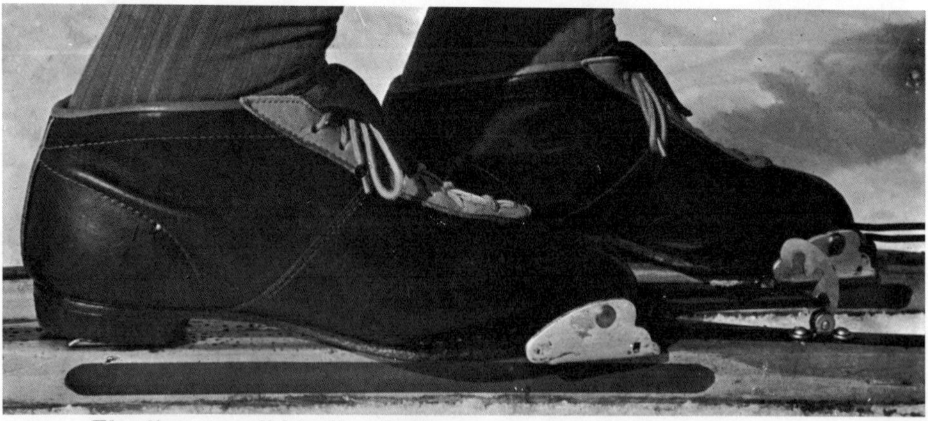

The "rat trap" binding is the most popular for cross-country skis. The heels are not attached so that you can raise or lower them freely for the stride.

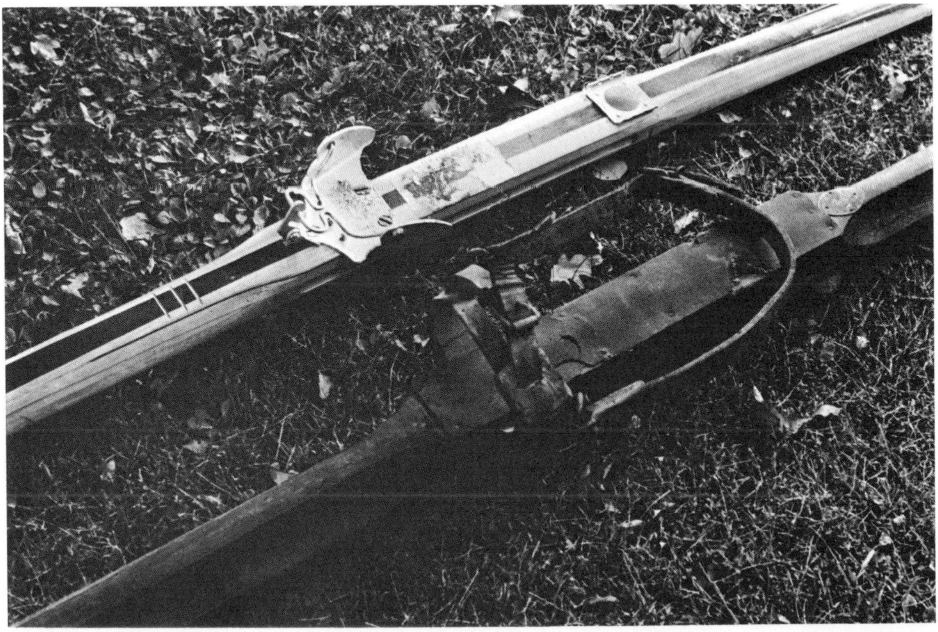

Modern bindings compared with one from the early 1900's.

to ascend, bending the foot, or else it can be fastened at the level of the heel for going downhill (this binding would be too heavy for racing).

You may wonder how the rat trap works going down an incline since it doesn't lock the heel. Stability in descent, especially at high speed, isn't compromised so much by the fact that the binding doesn't hold the shoe at the back as that the skis are narrower and lighter than downhill skis. In the last few years, some cross-country skiers have adopted the habit of screwing a metal plate onto their skis below the heel of their boot. The two side edges of the plate are raised and, with use, make corresponding cuts in the heel assuring greater general stability, especially in descent.

BOOTS

Cross-country boots should be light, soft and not too high. A pair of boots for racing doesn't weigh much more than a pair of ordinary walking shoes. The uninitiated may wonder how it is possible to do descents with such a light boot. Again the answer is in the balance between advantage and disadvantage. The disadvantage of trying to run on a flat course or accomplish a hard ascent wearing heavy boots is so great that the comparative disadvantage of light boots in a descent is practically nil. The disadvantages of using uncomfortable or heavy equipment can be overcome only by the improvement of technique.

Cross-country boots must fit perfectly. If they are small they ruin your feet, particularly your big toes. If they are too big they can form creases that end up painfully cutting your whole foot. The latest model boots are made of very fine leather, such as kangaroo skin, that doesn't do any damage if it creases.

Skiers normally wear one pair of woollen socks, knee length, of medium thickness. Under or even over the wool socks they also wear a pair of thin socks to protect feet from the cold as well as from blisters. This protection of the lower extremities is sufficient even when the temperature is very low. Athletes who are sensitive to the cold may also wear rubber overshoes when skiing in "polar" temperatures.

When it is raining or when there is a great deal of humidity, the overshoes do keep the feet dry. With wet feet, it is an easy matter to develop blisters. If you wear heavy wool socks or overshoes, you must pay attention that you don't lose your skis.

Cross-country boots must have low tops so that it is possible for you to bend your ankles. If your ankle is imprisoned in a high shoe, you are

Modern boots and bindings for cross-country and downhill skiing.

prevented from doing the necessary movements, in particular those for pushing. A boot for cross-country touring can be stronger and have a slightly higher top to give your feet better protection from the cold. A higher shoe also improves your stability and balance.

POLES

Poles for downhill skiing are usually made of metal or fiberglass. For cross-country competition, those of metal are too heavy and, in general, downhill poles are unsuitable because of their rigidity. How many times does a cross-country racer sink his poles into the snow during a 50-km. (30-mile) race? Certainly very many times. Therefore, if the poles are rigid, over the long run the arms that push them become more tired than normal and each planting of the pole is transformed into acute suffering. This is how it used to happen with the "Chinese water torture," with drops falling continuously on the head of the prisoner. After a while each drop on the skull produces the same suffering as a hammer blow.

The choice of one pole over another is strictly up to the individual. The important thing is that they are flexible, so as not to tire the arms unnecessarily.

The top part of the pole consists of a grip made of light material in a shape suitable for the hand. It includes a leather loop through which you pass your hand before gripping the pole so that you don't lose it during motion. If you don't do this the right way, it is impossible to use the poles properly.

The tip of the poles for downhill can be in the shape of a cone, but for cross-country it is better if the point is slightly hooked because this sticks less in hard-packed snow or ice (and there is less danger that it will break). The small wheel that keeps the poles from sinking into deep snow should not be very large and must be made of strong material. In recent years they have considered making it of plastic, but this material is inclined to break easily at low temperature.

The correct size of the poles varies from person to person and also depends somewhat on your style. There is, however, a general rule: stuck in the ground, a pole should come up to your armpit. Some skiers prefer

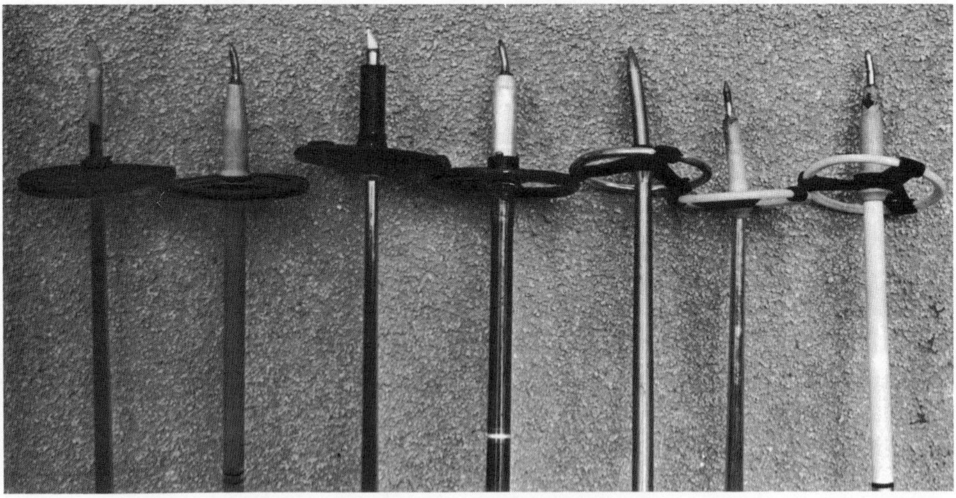

Poles are made of steel, bamboo and other materials. The tip is slightly hooked on a cross-country pole, making it less likely to stick in hard-packed snow or ice.

Pass your hand through the leather loop at the top of the pole before taking hold of the grip.

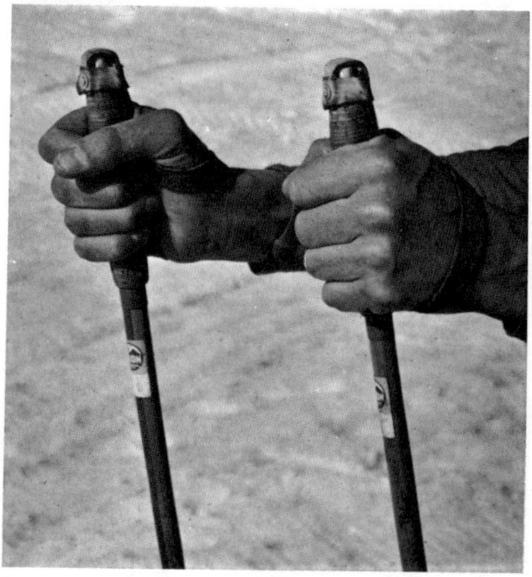

Grasp the poles firmly as you plant them in the snow.

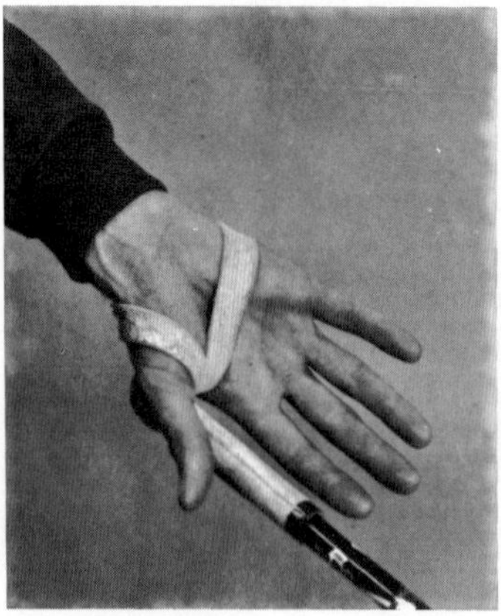

Allow your hand to open freely at the end of the backward swing following each push.

them longer, others shorter, so you need to try them each way until you find the size that works best for you. Somewhat longer poles may be called for on hard, fast courses on which you use double poling with a stride. With abundant, soft snow, long poles sink in too far and it is difficult to pull them out again. Poles that are too short force the legs and back muscles to work more and don't allow you to take advantage of the full capability of your arms. The opposite happens with poles that are too long which cause the arms to tire more than necessary. In cross-country skiing, the muscles should all work to their full potential but not be forced beyond.

CLOTHING

A cross-country racer wears pants that end just below the knee. They should be rather narrow in order not to give wind resistance, but not tight because they would then give less protection from the cold and would restrict your freedom of movement. Below the knee, the pants should tighten over the socks with a buckle or elastic. Don't tighten them too much or you will cut off the blood circulation. Racing pants have one or

For competition, a skier wears knee-length pants, wool socks, a light sweater, gloves, and a cap.

two pockets in the back to carry handkerchiefs and the necessities of ski wax. The pants should not be tight at the waist either, because the diaphragm and stomach must be completely free so you can breathe deeply during exertion. Underneath, a skier wears long, light underwear. Your thigh muscles must be kept warm to avoid cramps. When the temperature isn't excessively cold, you can race without the long underwear, especially if your pants are made of warm enough fabric.

On top, you wear an undershirt with long sleeves made of cotton or thin wool to absorb perspiration. Over this goes a racing sweater of wool, silk, nylon, or waterproof fabric. Two layers are generally enough, but in low temperatures you can add another thin undershirt, possibly without sleeves. Again, your clothes should not be too tight or too loose. Gloves are of thin, light leather with full or half fingers and, if it is very cold, they should be lined. Gloves also protect your hands in case of a hard fall. You are not required to wear gloves, but it is better to be prudent than to find yourself in a race with frozen hands.

Racing clothing is not warm enough to protect a skier from the cold while he is waiting for the race to begin. An easily removable warm-up suit will solve this problem.

Your head also needs to be protected from the cold. A skier should wear a cap, also light, so that his ears will be completely protected when the temperature is very low.

The gear described above, with some slight possible variation, is what a skier uses for racing. It is not suitable for slower touring in the mountains nor would it protect an athlete from the cold before or after the race. For these occasions, competitors should be equipped with a "warm-up suit" consisting of jacket and pants that are easy to put on and take off. The jacket pockets provide room for a cap and a pair of gloves heavier than those for racing which you should wear before the race and after having crossed the finish line.

You might wonder about using ordinary ski pants. These are excellent for touring, but in a race they are too tight and—because they are put down into the boots—can cause blisters on your heels. Touring fans can use some type of garment to protect them from the cold, but which still allows them freedom of movement, yet without covering them to the point where they perspire. It is a good idea to carry a change of clothes in a back pack, especially if you anticipate a long, tiring tour.

Young people who want to embrace the career of a cross-country skier should not think that all the equipment illustrated is indispensable in order to begin training or even to take part in a race. You can, of course, use the garments you already own that come closest to those described. With time you will complete the "required" outfit. It isn't only with equipment that you win a race; the main credit goes to the individual and his will power.

Waxing

Now we come to one of the most difficult aspects of cross-country skiing—waxing.

Wax hasn't changed much in recent years. Manufacturers have improved some of them, but still more or less the same waxes are sold in every sporting goods store. What has changed, however, is the bottom of the skis. Various types of waxless skis are at their best in certain types of snow. However, for the present, a ski that is waxed just right will be faster.

For the beginning and intermediate skiers, and those not interested in serious competition, the waxless skis eliminate a great deal of the time, effort and guesswork traditional to the sport. The more common waxable fiberglass skis still eliminate some effort by not using a base wax. It is not difficult to clean them after the race. Don't heat the fiberglass bottoms too much with the torch (see pages 131-132). It is easier to use wax remover to clean them.

For the time being, however, the cost of the various fiberglass skis may be prohibitive for the beginning or recreational cross-country skier. Wooden skis are still very popular and much less expensive, and it is not necessary to abandon old equipment. For this reason, what follows is the complete process of waxing. The dealer or manufacturer should be consulted for the proper care of the skis.

For a downhill skier, the purpose of waxing is to prepare the skis so that they create as little friction as possible in descent. Going back up is no problem, since these skiers use mechanical lifts to reascend. The original cross-country skiers used a piece of seal skin wrapped around one ski to push themselves uphill, a method that is too cumbersome and complicated for cross-country racer or touring skier. For this, modern cross-country skiers use a different type of wax.

Any racing team needs an assortment of waxes, irons to spread the wax, and a collection of corks, torches and other materials for cleaning the bottom of their skis.

Wax is divided into "grundvalla" (ground or base wax) and surface wax. Grundvalla (the original Scandinavian names are used internationally) serves to impregnate and protect the bottom of the ski and to allow the surface wax to adhere. The term "wax" by itself generally means surface wax. This gives the ski maximum forward speed, but also causes it to adhere to the snow when the skier pushes with his leg, whether on flat ground or going up inclines.

So far no one has invented a "universal" wax, suitable for every type of snow. The snow crystals that penetrate the wax prevent the ski from sliding backwards by changing their structure with the changes of temperature. The snow in its turn gets cold and dry, damp, wet, frozen or assumes many other states. Therefore, it is necessary to find a type of wax of such consistency that the snow crystals adhere to the skis in sufficient measure to allow them to slide forward, but prevent them from sliding backwards. If too many snow crystals adhere to the wax, they form a lump which impedes forward motion. If they don't adhere at all, the ski slides backwards.

THE ORIGINS

In the past, when, in the Scandinavian countries at the end of the long summer rest, a skier went down to the cellar to bring up his skis, the air was completely filled with the aroma of tar—a strong smell that tugged at your heart since it brought back memories of racing the preceding winter and made you think about what was awaiting you in the near future. But you remembered also the summer just passed, because the boats that were used during the summer on the lakes and along the rivers were also soaked with tar.

With skis in hand again, summer was quickly forgotten. Examining the bottoms of the skis you might see streaks of raw wood amid the tar burned into the wood. If these streaks were few, you could immediately begin skiing, satisfied with the coating. If there were, instead, many patches of raw wood, you had to work for an hour with torch and tar—a difficult task. Eventually, tar covered the bottom of the skis again, but it had also dirtied faces and the floor of the cellar.

This "waxing," although primitive, was enough for half the winter and was used for every type of snow. On days when the snow caked under the skis or the skis slid backwards, you preferred not to ski. The slyer ones, when the snow caked, remedied it with a handful of paraffin or suet, confining it to the back part of the ski. Many people remember this device of waxing only half of the ski with paraffin, and some of them—erroneously—use modern wax in the same way.

In the past, on the occasion of the most important races, you often heard talk about "magicians" who used a magic blend to defeat their adversaries. These magicians surrounded themselves with mystery, but really they had found the basis for the composition of wax that is used today.

At first the various mixtures all had a tar base, and so little skiers all had dirty finger nails all winter. Since then, many things have changed and the smell of tar doesn't hang over Nordic skiers any more. Modern waxes are produced chemically, and those few tars that you still find leave little aroma or hardly dirty your hands.

To learn to wax you have to go along the course, observe, touch the snow, be capable of judging the temperature of the air and snow, anticipate possible changes in temperature and in the state of the snow, and many other things. No one can become an absolute expert, even if today it is possible to find waxes for each type of snow. Maybe it is just the uncertainty over the choice of wax, even among the great champions, that leaves the outcome of a competition open and adds one more measure of interest to the race.

GRUNDVALLA

Competitors today can obtain racing skis already prepared with grundvalla at the factory (they are skis to be used within a short time). In general, new pairs of skis have a protective coating on the bottoms to prevent excessive drying out in the store. When a skier buys a pair of new skis not yet prepared with grundvalla, he should scrape off the bottom coating completely using sandpaper or steel wool, then apply the grundvalla.

The traditional method of applying grundvalla is to use a blow torch or some other apparatus that gives heat to warm the tar without burning it, making it penetrate the wood. Today, some skiers don't do it this way but, instead, heat a base wax on the clean bottom and then polish it energetically. It is difficult to say which method produces the best base. Maybe the old method is still the surest for most types of snow.

When you put grundvalla on a pair of skis for the first time you must be careful not to heat the wood too much, because the skis may be deformed (that is, warp or acquire too much camber) or else the bottom can be charred and the ski ruined. It is better to apply several light coats of grundvalla, one at a time.

A word of advice to beginners in the use of the blow torch: always start warming the ski in the middle where it is thicker, then work towards the

The first step in preparing your skis is to spread "grundvalla" or base wax over the bottom.

You can either heat the base wax with a torch to make it penetrate into the wood or heat the wax with an iron and polish it energetically with cloth.

tip and the tail. So far as possible, hold the source of heat perpendicular to the ski and directed to the middle of it. Spread grundvalla on the ski with a brush, but not too much at one time. Wipe off any grundvalla that isn't absorbed by the wood using a cotton rag (not newspaper). It is better to apply grundvalla indoors and it is a wise idea to protect the floor with a sheet of paper. You will be able to work easily if you rest the skis on a pair of sawhorses.

If you see that the camber has increased too much after applying the grundvalla, tie the skis together in several places and let them cool that way. If, instead, the camber is too shallow, put a piece of wood between the skis in the middle and tie them together.

Finally, clean the skis well on the top and sides. When you expect to find fresh snow it is important that the grundvalla be perfectly dry to prevent ice from forming on the bottom of the skis.

Grundvalla cannot be used on skis with plastic bottoms. For this kind of ski you do sometimes use a base wax.

THE DIFFERENT WAXES

Before a race, a competitor should have two pairs of skis prepared with grundvalla, but not the other wax. Waxing takes some time and if a skier is sure enough about the snow conditions the evening before, he can risk waxing one pair with the wax he thinks is going to be suitable.

The snow can change during the night and this way he will have to have another unwaxed pair available on the morning of the race.

Many different brands of wax are offered for sale, perhaps too many.

Swix, made in Sweden and Norway, Ex-elit from Sweden, Rex from Finland and the Italian Rode are among the most commonly used, but there are other famous brands as well, and it is impossible to say which is the best. A skier should not, however, jump from one brand to another, race after race: it is better to concentrate on one or two brands and to learn to use these as well as possible.

Remember that the speed on the course doesn't depend as much on the type of wax as on the way it is applied. The major brands generally follow the same color-code scheme—green Rode, for example, is intended for the same type of snow as the green Swix, and so on. Naturally, even between two similar types some differences do exist, just enough that on a particular day it just might lead to victory in a race.

Some manufacturers also produce wax for downhill skiing and this can sometimes be used for cross-country, but it seldom happens. In addition, it is a good idea to spread some paraffin on the sides and the upper surfaces of the skis so that snow doesn't stick to them.

THE BASIC GROUPS

The waxes can be divided into five basic groups:

(1) grundvalla is a base to protect the skis and to make the running wax adhere;

(2) hard wax for cold atmospheric temperatures;

(3) soft wax for temperatures around 0° C. (32° F.) or a little above;

(4) soft klister for fairly warm temperatures;

(5) viscous or "sticky" klister for ice.

WHAT WAX TO USE

1. GRUNDVALLA, BASE

Rode grundvalla—heat to impregnate the bottom and make the running wax adhere.

Rode black base—use as a base for hard wax when you foresee notable use.

Rode paste—base for klister.

2. HARD WAX

Rode special green—for very cold temperatures.

Rode green—dry snow, cold temperatures: —5° C. (23° F.) or less.

Rode blue—dry snow from 0° to −5° C. (23–32° F.).

The correct wax to use depends upon the outside temperature and the condition of the snow.

Apply surface wax by rubbing the stick directly on the ski.

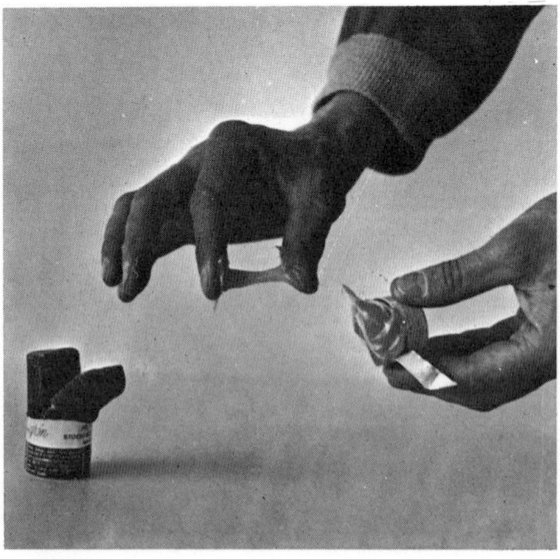

Some creamy waxes are available in tubes.

3. SOFT WAX
   Rode purple—slightly damp snow, temperature around 0° C. (32° F.).
   Rode yellow—wet snow, temperature above 0° C. (32° F.).
4. SOFT KLISTER
   Rode red klister—wet snow, high temperature.
   Rode purple klister—wet icy snow.
   Rode silver klister—very wet or melting snow.
5. VISCOUS KLISTER
   Rode skare—for frozen courses.

SOME EXAMPLES

If two skiers of equal weight put on the same wax and you see that out on the track one is consistently faster than the other, this can be due to the fact that the slower of the two has put on too much wax. In fact, a large amount of wax makes the skis adhere well for ascent, but impedes the forward glide. A small amount of wax makes the skis faster, but you risk sliding backwards. For this reason, you must try your skis out before a race—even then it may be better if you wax two pairs of skis, one more heavily than the other, to see which has the right amount.

Wax is applied in very thin layers. Modern wax is a chemical compound and is warmed on the bottom of the ski with an iron. Then you smooth it out with a cork or other suitable material, and this is a very important operation. Besides the warming iron and a cork, you will need a scraper to wipe off excess wax or eventual incrustations of ice.

When the temperature is below freezing and the snow is cold, there are no problems; Rode green is excellent. Often, however, it isn't possible to use a single wax and you have to combine several types. For example, with a temperature of −5° C. (+23° F.) the green glides well, but you tend to slide backwards. If you apply more of the green, you compromise the gliding ahead, but the skis slide backwards just the same. In this case it is better to put a shadow of blue on top of the green or to apply the blue only in the middle of the ski. Maybe the skis won't be quite as fast as before, but it does adhere better to the snow. If a cover of fresh snow falls on an icy track, you cannot do anything without Rode skare. Yet you notice that the skis don't glide well because of the fresh snow. You can improve this situation by putting a little of the green or blue over the skare.

The competitor who goes to test his racing skis in fresh snow should not ski just a short distance, but should try them for at least 10 minutes. More-

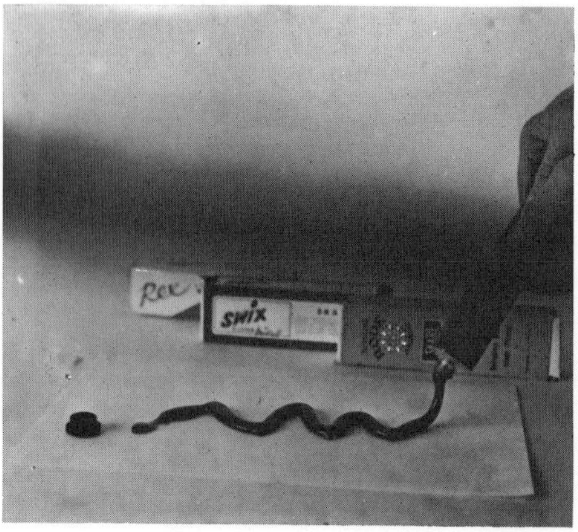

Apply cream wax from a tube directly to the ski.

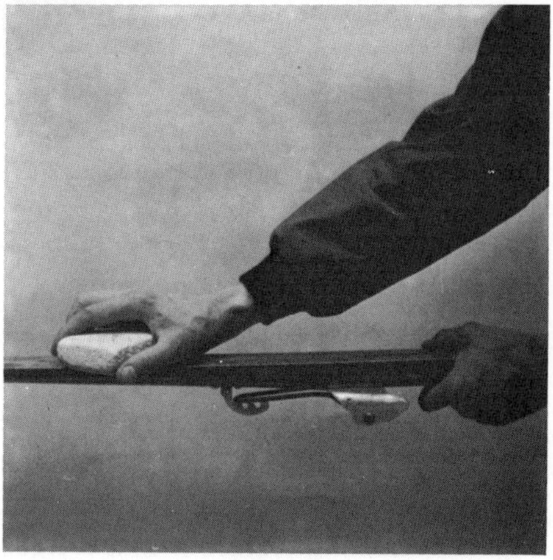

Use a cork to spread the wax evenly over the surface.

over, the competitor should survey the whole race course, not just the starting and finish lines. In many races you start out under a bright sun that makes the track wet, then the course goes higher into cold, fresh snow, and possibly the end is transformed into an icy track. In this case you really must use your head.

There are many possible problems and combinations of them and for each one you have to seek the best combination of waxes. Waxing is easier for the ski tourer than for the competitors in a race; they don't have the need to rush and can take the time to apply one wax in the morning and later, if necessary, change it along the way. Changing wax during a race, however, is something you very seldom see.

Useful advice for a ski touring skier is: better to put on a wax that is too hard than one that is too soft. Perhaps hard wax lets you slip backwards a little, but it is easier to cover a hard wax than a soft one. It is more difficult to put hard wax over soft, in case you find cold snow: first you would have to scrape the skis.

Here is some useful advice for young racers:

(1) start waxing well before departure time;

(2) always take two pairs of skis;

(3) test out your skis yourself, don't have someone else try them;

(4) don't try out just a short stretch of the course, but continue for a distance;

(5) ask the advice of your trainer or other skiers, but in the end decide for yourself;

(6) when your decision is firmly made, don't go around looking at what others have done;

(7) check the evening before the race to see if the torch, wax and the rest of the material are in order.

Characteristics of Cross-Country Races

Time and the evolution of skiing have led to today's official racing distances ranging from the very fast "15 kilometre" to the more cautious "30 kilometre" up to the very tiring "50 kilometre," true marathons of skiing. Even longer distances are still contested today (it is enough to mention the well known "Wasalopp," 87 km. long), but in the most important meets, such as the Olympic Games and the World Championships, only the official distances are run, plus the women's races (of 5 and 10 km.) and the two relays, men's (4×10 km.) and women's (4×5 km.).

The racing terrain is also being standardized according to international criteria. The modern layout of tracks is suitable for teaching Scandinavian type skiing. Today they include a mixed, rolling terrain without steep inclines. The "Technical Regulations for Ski Races," published by FIS (the International Federation of Skiing), establishes that the maximum incline between the lowest and highest points may not exceed 100 metres for the women's 5-km. race; 150 metres for the women's 10-km. and the 10-km. for juniors; 200 metres for the men's 10-km. (juniors' 15-km.); and 250 metres for the men's 15-km. or greater. The incline of a "maximum ascent" may not exceed 75 metres for the women's trials and 100 metres for the men's.

It is interesting to note that the Italian Association, taking as a model the guiding Scandinavian system, in fixing types and inclines of the racing courses, tries to ensure that "the cross-country race course is for the competitors a true test of power, strength, skiing technique, and of tactical ability in racing." To obtain this result, it specifies that ascents, descents, and flat terrain are divided into approximately equal parts, that the course is laid out over the terrain in a natural and varied way without artificial obstacles, without long and monotonous runs, without ascents that are too steep and difficult and without dangerous descents; that the initial run doesn't compel the competitor to use exaggerated effort too soon, that the most demanding part is in the middle; that the course, as a whole, avoiding sharp turns and changes of direction, allows the competitors to maintain the rhythm of the full gait.

In international races, skiers are divided into four groups: for the first part the IV group, and for the last part the I. The competitors must follow the laid-out course and pass by all the control posts; they cannot use means of propelling themselves other than with their own skis and poles; they cannot be followed on the course by non-competitors, neither can anyone but competitors be alongside them nor ahead of them; the entire course must be covered with skis on feet, skis that must be marked before departure; if a ski or binding breaks, the competitor is authorized to change the ski, but must pass the finish line with at least one of the original marked skis. On the other hand, he can change as many broken poles as he wants; he can stop to adjust his skis or broken bindings or to wax on the condition that he doesn't receive assistance from anyone else. During the run he can accept refreshment and receive information about his position in the race and about the other competitors. At the first request, an overtaken athlete must leave the course open to allow the other competitor to pass.

The rules must be observed in a sportsmanlike way. It is in the interest of every athlete, trainer and assistant always to be informed and up-to-date concerning the regulations.

The Great World Champions

This volume, dedicated to the technique of cross-country skiing, closes with a brief review of the greatest champions of this sport. Each of them, in his time, created a new style of racing, has made his mark in the evolution of Nordic skiing.

Thorleif Haug, born in Norway in 1894, was the first great cross-country champion in the modern sense. He excelled in all the Nordic events at the first running of the Olympic Winter Games in 1924.

Veikko Hakulinen of Finland is one of the few cross-country skiers to perform well in four successive runnings of the Olympic Winter Games.

To the great Scandinavian names can now be added, with good reason, skiers from other countries, who have had success in the last few years in their own lands and others, even without having a tradition for this type of skiing in their background, nor a large pool of athletes from which to select the members of the national team.

Thanks to the skill of these champions and to the publicity that the sport has generated, many people all over the world have started to "ski as in the North." May the examples of the champions and the suggestions in this book make their path easier and smoother running.

Giulio de Florian has been one of Italy's leading contenders in international competition.

Ero Maentyranta of Finland is the smiling skier who brought excitement to the cross-country events at the 1964 Winter Games in Innsbruck, Austria—the very heart of downhill skiing territory.

Index